BEGIN
again

Also by Max Lucado

Inspirational

3:16

A Gentle Thunder

A Love Worth Giving

And the Angels Were Silent

Anxious for Nothing

Because of Bethlehem

Before Amen

Come Thirsty

Cure for the Common Life

Facing Your Giants

Fearless

Glory Days

God Came Near

Grace

Great Day Every Day

He Chose the Nails

He Still Moves Stones

How Happiness Happens

In the Eye of the Storm

In the Grip of Grace

It's Not About Me

Jesus

Just Like Jesus

Max on Life

More to Your Story

Next Door Savior

No Wonder They Call
Him the Savior

On the Anvil

Outlive Your Life

Six Hours One Friday

The Applause of Heaven

The Great House of God

Traveling Light

Unshakable Hope

When Christ Comes

When God Whispers
Your Name

You Are Never Alone

You'll Get Through This

Fiction

Christmas Stories

Miracle at the Higher
Grounds Café

The Christmas Candle

Bibles (General Editor)

The Lucado Encouraging
Word Bible

Children's Daily
Devotional Bible

Grace for the Moment
Daily Bible

The Lucado Life
Lessons Study Bible

Children's Books

A Max Lucado
Children's Treasury

Do You Know I
Love You, God?

God Always Keeps
His Promises

God Forgives Me,
and I Forgive You

God Listens When I Pray

Grace for the Moment:
365 Devotions for Kids

Hermie, a Common
Caterpillar

I'm Not a Scaredy Cat

Itsy Bitsy Christmas

Just in Case You
Ever Wonder

Lucado Treasury of
Bedtime Prayers

One Hand, Two Hands

Thank You, God,
for Blessing Me

Thank You, God,
for Loving Me

The Boy and the Ocean

The Crippled Lamb

The Oak Inside the Acorn

The Tallest of Smalls

You Are Mine

You Are Special

Young Adult Books

3:16

It's Not About Me

Make Every Day Count

Wild Grace

You Were Made to
Make a Difference

Gift Books

Fear Not Promise Book

For the Tough Times

God Thinks You're
Wonderful

Grace for the Moment

Grace Happens Here

Happy Today

His Name Is Jesus

Let the Journey Begin

Live Loved

Mocha with Max

Safe in the Shepherd's Arms

This Is Love

You Changed My Life

BEGIN
again

Your Hope and Renewal Start Today

MAX LUCADO

THOMAS NELSON
Since 1798

To Jack and Deb Graham and O. S. and Susie Hawkins.
The completion of this book coincides with the
commemoration of fifty years of marriage and
ministry for each of these wonderful couples.
We celebrate their devotion to Jesus and each other.

Published in Nashville, Tennessee, by Thomas Nelson. Thomas Nelson is a registered trademark of HarperCollins Christian Publishing, Inc.

Thomas Nelson titles may be purchased in bulk for educational, business, fund-raising, or sales promotional use. For information, please e-mail SpecialMarkets@ThomasNelson.com.

Unless otherwise noted, Scripture quotations are taken from the Holy Bible, New International Version®, NIV®. Copyright © 1973, 1978, 1984, 2011 by Biblica, Inc.™ Used by permission of Zondervan. All rights reserved worldwide. www.zondervan.com. The "NIV" and "New International Version" are trademarks registered in the United States Patent and Trademark Office by Biblica, Inc.™

Scripture quotations marked AMP are from the Amplified® Bible. Copyright © 1954, 1958, 1962, 1964, 1965, 1987 by The Lockman Foundation. Used by permission. (www.Lockman.org)

Scripture quotations marked ESV are from the ESV® Bible (The Holy Bible, English Standard Version®). Copyright © 2001 by Crossway, a publishing ministry of Good News Publishers. Used by permission. All rights reserved.

Scripture quotations marked GNT are from the Good News Translation in Today's English Version—Second Edition. Copyright 1992 by American Bible Society. Used by permission.

Scripture quotations marked THE MESSAGE are from *The Message*. Copyright © by Eugene H. Peterson 1993, 1994, 1995, 1996, 2000, 2001, 2002. Used by permission of Tyndale House Publishers, Inc.

Scripture quotations marked NASB are from the New American Standard Bible®. Copyright © 1960, 1962, 1963, 1968, 1971, 1972, 1973, 1975, 1977, 1995 by The Lockman Foundation. Used by permission. (www.Lockman.org)

Scripture quotations marked NCV are from the New Century Version®. © 2005 by Thomas Nelson. Used by permission. All rights reserved.

Scripture quotations marked NEB are from the New English Bible. © Cambridge University Press and Oxford University Press 1961, 1970. All rights reserved.

Scripture quotations marked NKJV are from the New King James Version®. © 1982 by Thomas Nelson. Used by permission. All rights reserved.

Scripture quotations marked NLT are from the *Holy Bible*, New Living Translation. © 1996, 2004, 2007, 2013, 2015 by Tyndale House Foundation. Used by permission of Tyndale House Publishers, Inc., Carol Stream, Illinois 60188. All rights reserved.

Scripture quotations marked NLV are from the *New Life Version*. © 1969 and 2003. Used by permission of Barbour Publishing, Inc., Uhrichsville, Ohio 44683. All rights reserved.

Scripture quotations marked NRSV are from the New Revised Standard Version Bible. Copyright © 1989 National Council of the Churches of Christ in the United States of America. Used by permission. All rights reserved.

Scripture quotations marked PHILLIPS are from THE NEW TESTAMENT IN MODERN ENGLISH, Revised Edition, © J. B. Phillips 1958, 1960, 1972. Used by permission of Macmillan Publishing Co., Inc.

Scriptures marked TLB are from *The Living Bible*. Copyright © 1971. Used by permission of Tyndale House Publishers, Inc., Carol Stream, Illinois 60188. All rights reserved.

Any Internet addresses, phone numbers, or company or product information printed in this book are offered as a resource and are not intended in any way to be or to imply an endorsement by Thomas Nelson, nor does Thomas Nelson vouch for the existence, content, or services of these sites, phone numbers, companies, or products beyond the life of this book.

ISBN 978-1-4002-2649-8 (eBook)
ISBN 978-1-4002-2647-4 (HC)
ISBN 978-1-4002-2674-0 (IE)

Library of Congress Control Number: 2020941582

Printed in the United States of America
20 21 22 23 24 LSC 10 9 8 7 6 5 4 3 2 1

Contents

Acknowledgments   ix

Introduction: Catch a Glimpse of New Possibilities   xi

PART 1: BELIEVE YOUR TRUSTWORTHY GOD   1

  1. Trust Your Shepherd   5
  2. Give Your Fears to Your Father   11
  3. Seeing with Eyes Closed   15
  4. Don't Give Up   23
  5. Follow the God Who Follows You   31

PART 2: ENJOY GOD'S GOOD GIFTS   39

  6. Accept the Gift of Himself   43
  7. Rely On the Holy Spirit   51
  8. Shelter in His Protection   57
  9. Settle Down Deep in His Love   65

PART 3: GROUND YOURSELF IN HIS PROMISES   73

  10. Hold On to Your Soul Anchor   77
  11. Choose Faith   87
  12. Let Your Father Fight for You   93
  13. Keep Believing God's Promise   99

CONTENTS

PART 4: INFLUENCE YOUR WORLD   103

14. Be You   107
15. Share What God Has Given   111
16. Love Those in Need   119
17. Make a Difference   125

PART 5: NURTURE AN ETERNAL PERSPECTIVE   129

18. Reserve Judgment of Life's Storms   131
19. Chronicle What Christ Has Done   137
20. Listen for the Song of the Whip-poor-will   143
Epilogue: A Final Word   147

Questions for Reflection   151

Sources   211

Notes   215

Acknowledgments

When I think about the people who made this book happen, I think about some of the finest people I have ever known. Joey Paul, Janene MacIvor, Karen Hill, Carol Bartley, Andrea Lucado, Greg and Susan Ligon, Steve and Cheryl Green, Mark Glesne, Erica Smith, Tim Paulson, and Don Jacobson. To each of you, thank you.

Introduction

Catch a Glimpse of New Possibilities

Water. All Noah can see is water. The evening sun sinks into it. The clouds are reflected in it. His boat is surrounded by it. Water. Water to the north. Water to the south. Water to the east. Water to the west. Water.

All Noah can see is water.

He can't remember when he's seen anything but. The world has been destroyed. It was the end of everything he had known. He and the boys had barely pushed the last hippo up the ramp when heaven opened a thousand fire hydrants. Within moments the boat was rocking, and for days the rain was pouring, and for weeks Noah has been wondering, *How long is this going to last?* For forty days it has rained. For months they have floated. They have eaten the same food, smelled the same smells, and looked at the same faces. After a certain point you run out of things to say to each other. You even begin to run low on hope. *Can God re-create this world? Is he able to start over? Can he, and we, begin again?*

Finally the boat bumped, and the rocking stopped. Mrs. Noah gave Mr. Noah a look, and Noah gave the hatch a shove and poked his head through. The hull of the ark was resting on ground, but the ground was still surrounded by water. "Noah," she yelled up at him, "what do you see?"

"Water."

He sent a raven on a scouting mission; it never returned. He sent a dove. It came back shivering and spent, having found no place to roost. Then, just this morning, he tried again. He pulled a dove out of the bowels of the ark and ascended the ladder. The morning sun caused them both to squint. As he kissed the breast of the bird, he felt a pounding heart. Had he put a hand on his chest, he would have felt another. With a prayer he let it go and watched until the bird was no bigger than a speck.

All day he looked for the dove's return. In between chores he opened the hatch and searched. The boys wanted him to play a little pin the tail on the donkey, but he passed. He chose instead to climb into the crow's nest and look. The wind lifted his gray hair. The sun warmed his weather-beaten face. But nothing lifted his heavy heart. He had seen nothing. Not in the morning. Not after lunch. Not later.

Now the sun is setting, and the sky is darkening, and he has come to look one final time, but all he sees is water. Water to the north. Water to the south. Water to the east. Water to the . . .

You know the feeling. You have stood where Noah stood. You've known your share of floods. Flooded by sorrow at the cemetery, anger at the disability in your body, fear of the uncertainty of a pandemic. You've seen the floodwater rise, and you've likely seen the sun set on your hopes and dreams as well. You've been on Noah's boat.

And you've needed what Noah needed; you've needed hope. Hope doesn't promise an instant solution but rather the possibility of an eventual one. Sometimes all we need is a little hope.

That's all Noah needed. And that's what Noah received.

The old sailor stares at the sun bisected by the horizon. One could hardly imagine a more beautiful sight. But he'd give this one and a hundred more for an acre of dry ground and a grove of grapes. Mrs. Noah's voice reminds him that dinner is on the table and he should lock the hatch, and he's just about to call it a day when he hears the cooing of the dove. This is how the Bible describes the moment: "When the dove returned to him in the evening, there in its beak was a freshly plucked olive leaf!" (Gen. 8:11).

An olive leaf. Noah would have been happy to have the bird—but to have the leaf! This leaf was more than foliage; this was promise. The bird brought more than a piece of a tree; it brought hope. For isn't that what hope is? Hope is an olive leaf—evidence of dry land after a flood. Proof to the dreamer that dreaming is worth the risk.

Are you in need of some hope? Could you use a fresh start? A redo? A mulligan? At some point in life we all could. The oh-so-welcome news of Scripture is this: God is a God of fresh starts. He is the author of the new chapter, the architect of the new design, the voice behind the new song.

God knows the way forward. No matter what kind of disappointment or grief or trouble or heartache you've encountered, God offers an opportunity to begin again. In his plan prodigals get a new robe, the weary find new strength, and the lonely find a friend.

> Those who wait on the LORD
> Shall renew their strength;
> They shall mount up with wings like eagles,
> They shall run and not be weary,
> They shall walk and not faint. (Isa. 40:31 NKJV)

Your current circumstances will not get the final say in your life.

To all the Noahs of the world, to all who search the horizon for a glimpse of hope, God proclaims, "Yes!" And he comes. He comes as a dove. He comes bearing fruit from a distant land, from our future home. He comes with a leaf of promise that he can make all things new.

That is the theme of the book you hold, a combination of new thoughts and some favorite ones from prior books. The theme is simply this: Your hope can be restored. Your dreams can be renewed. By God's grace you can find your way to dry land, watch the waters subside, and step out on fresh soil.

With God as your guide, you can begin again.

part one

Believe Your
Trustworthy God

My dad decorated our den with a stump. I was just a kid at the time, eleven years old, maybe twelve. The perfect age to be fascinated with the idea of a tree stump sitting next to the fireplace.

Over the fireplace, a clock.

Next to the fireplace, fireplace tools.

Next to the tools, a stump.

Awesome.

He came home from work with it one day. It took up the better portion of the bed of his pickup. That's where it lay when I first saw it. Dad pulled it out of his truck and let it fall onto the concrete driveway.

"What is it, Dad?"

"It's a tree stump," he answered with no small amount of pride.

Dad worked in the oil fields of West Texas. It was his job to make sure the pump machinery functioned smoothly. Apparently this tree trunk was interfering with his work. Quite honestly I don't remember why it troubled him. Perhaps it blocked his access to an engine. Maybe it leaned too far across a dirt path. Whatever the reason, it kept him from doing his work in the way he wanted to do it. So he yanked it out of the ground. He wrapped one end of a chain around the trunk and the other end around his trailer hitch. The contest was over before it began.

But dislodging the tree wasn't enough for him; he wanted to display it. Some men hang antlers on their walls. Others fill a room with deer heads or a taxidermied bass. My dad opted to decorate our den with a tree trunk.

Mom was less than enthused. As they stood on the driveway and exchanged animated opinions, I examined the bagged quarry. The trunk was as wide as my size twenty-nine waist. The bark had long since dried and was easy to peel away. Thumb-thick roots hung limp from the base. I've never considered myself to be a connoisseur of dead trees, but this much I knew: this trunk was a real beauty.

Over the years I've often reflected on my dad's decision to turn a trunk into decor, especially because I consider myself to be a tree trunk of my own making. When God found me, I was a fruitless stump with deep roots. I offered no beauty to the landscape of the world. No one found shade under my limbs. I even interfered with the work of the Father. Even so, he found a place for me. It required a good yank and no small amount of cleaning up, but he took me from badlands to his home and displayed me as a work of his own.

Such is the work of the Holy Spirit.

And we all, with unveiled face, beholding the glory of the Lord, are being transformed into the same image from one degree of glory to another. For this comes from the Lord who is the Spirit. (2 Cor. 3:18 ESV)

The Spirit of God will transform you into a handiwork of heaven and display you in full view. Expect to be scrubbed, sanded, and varnished a time or two or ten. But in the end the result will be worth the discomfort.

You'll be grateful.

In the end so was my mom. Remember the heated discussion my parents had about the stump? Dad won. He placed the stump in our den—but only after he cleaned it up, varnished it, and carved on it "Jack and Thelma" in big letters and the names of their four kids beneath. I can't speak for my siblings, but I was always proud to see my name on the family tree of a stump puller.

chapter one

Trust Your Shepherd

He restores my soul.
—PSALM 23:3 NKJV

Imagine yourself in a jungle. A dense jungle. A dark jungle. Your friends convinced you it was time for a once-in-a-lifetime trip, and here you are. You paid the fare. You crossed the ocean. You hired the guide and joined the group. And you ventured where you had never ventured before—into the thick, strange world of the jungle.

Sound interesting? Let's take it a step farther. Imagine that you are in the jungle, lost and alone. You paused to lace your boot, and when you looked up, no one was near. You took a chance and went to the right; now you're wondering if the others went to the left. (Or did you go left and they go right?)

Whatever, you are alone. And you have been alone for, well, you don't know how long it has been. Your watch was attached to your pack, and your pack is on the shoulder of the nice guy from New Jersey who volunteered to hold it while you tied your boots. You didn't intend for him to walk off with it. But he did. And here you are, stuck in the middle of nowhere.

You have a problem. First, you were not made for this place. Drop you into the center of avenues and buildings, and you could sniff your way home. But here in sky-blocking foliage? Here in trail-hiding thickets? You are out of your element. You weren't made for this jungle.

What's worse, you aren't equipped. You have no machete. No knife. No matches. No flares. No food. And now you are trapped—and you haven't a clue how to get out.

Sound like fun to you? Me neither. Before moving on let's pause and ask how you would feel. Given such circumstances, what emotions would surface? With what thoughts would you wrestle?

Fear? Of course you would.

Anxiety? To say the least.

Anger? I could understand that. (You'd like to get your hands on those folks who convinced you to take this trip.)

But most of all what about hopelessness? No idea where to turn. No hunch what to do. Who could blame you for sitting on a log (better check for snakes first), burying your face in your hands, and thinking, *I'll never get out of here*? You have no direction, no equipment, no hope.

Can you freeze-frame that emotion for a moment? Can you sense for just a second how it feels to be out of your element? Out of solutions? Out of ideas and energy? Can you imagine just for a moment how it feels to be out of hope?

If you can, you can relate to many people in this world.

For many people life is—well, life is a jungle. Not a jungle of trees and beasts. Would that it were so simple. Would that our jungles could be cut with a machete or our adversaries trapped in a cage. But our jungles are composed of the thicker thickets of contagious diseases, broken hearts, and empty wallets. Our forests are framed with hospital walls and divorce courts. We don't hear the screeching of birds or the roaring of lions, but we do hear the complaints of politicians and the demands of bosses. Our predators are our creditors, and the brush that surrounds us is the uncertainty that terrifies us.

It's a jungle out there.

And for some, even for many, hope is in short supply. Hopelessness is an odd bag. Unlike the others it isn't full. It is empty, and its emptiness creates the burden. Unzip the top and examine all the pockets. Turn it upside down and shake it hard. The bag of hopelessness is painfully empty.

Not a very pretty picture, is it? Let's see if we can brighten it up. We've imagined the emotions of being lost. Do you think we can do the same with being rescued? What would it take to restore your hope? What would you need to reenergize your journey?

Though the answers are abundant, three come quickly to mind.

The first would be a person. Not just any person. You don't need someone equally confused. You need someone who knows the way out. Someone you can trust.

And from him you need some vision. You need someone to lift your spirits. You need someone to look you in the face and say, "This isn't the end. Don't give up. You can begin again. There is a better place than this. And I'll lead you there."

And perhaps most important you need direction. If you have only a person but no renewed vision, all you have is company. If he has a vision

7

but no direction, you have a dreamer for company. But if you have a person with direction—who can take you from this place to the right place—ah, then you have one who can restore your hope.

Or, to use David's words, "He restores my soul" (Ps. 23:3 NKJV).

Our Shepherd majors in restoring hope to the soul. Whether you are a lamb lost on a craggy ledge or a city slicker alone in a deep jungle, everything changes when your rescuer appears.

Your loneliness diminishes because you have fellowship.

Your despair decreases because you have vision.

Your confusion begins to lift because you have direction.

Please note: you haven't left the jungle. The trees still eclipse the sky, and the thorns still cut the skin. Animals lurk and rodents scurry. The jungle is still a jungle. It hasn't changed, but you have. You have changed because your hope has been restored. And you have hope because you have met someone who can lead you out.

Your Shepherd knows that you were not made for this place. He knows you are not equipped for this place. So he has come to guide you out.

He is the perfect one to do so.

He has the right vision. He reminds you that "you are like foreigners and strangers in this world" (1 Peter 2:11 NCV). And he urges you to lift your eyes from the jungle around you to see the heaven above you. "Don't shuffle along, eyes to the ground, absorbed with the things right in front of you. Look up, and be alert to what is going on around Christ. . . . See things from *his* perspective" (Col. 3:2 THE MESSAGE).

David said it this way: "I lift up my eyes to the mountains—where does my help come from? My help comes from the LORD, the Maker of heaven and earth. He will not let your foot slip—he who watches over you will not slumber. . . . The LORD watches over you . . . the sun will not harm you by day, nor the moon by night. The LORD will keep you from all harm—he will watch over your life" (Ps. 121:1–3, 5–7).

God, your rescuer, has the right vision. He also has the right direction. He made the boldest claim in the history of humanity when he declared, "I am the way" (John 14:6). People wondered if the claim was accurate. He answered their questions by cutting a path through the underbrush of sin and death . . . and escaping alive. He's the only One who ever did. And he is the only One who can help you and me do the same.

He has the right vision: he has seen the homeland. He has the right directions: he has cut the path. But most of all he is the right person, because he is our God. Who knows the jungle better than the One who made it? And who knows the pitfalls of the path better than the One who has walked it?

The story is told of a man on an African safari deep in the jungle. The guide ahead of him had a machete and was whacking away the tall weeds and thick underbrush. The traveler, weary and hot, asked in frustration, "Where are we? Do you know where you are taking me? Where is the path?" The seasoned guide stopped and looked back at the man and replied, "I am the path."

We ask the same questions, don't we? We ask God, "Where are you taking me? Where is the path?" And he, like the guide, doesn't tell us. Oh, he may give us a hint or two, but that's all. If he did, would we understand? Would we comprehend our location? No, like the traveler, we are unacquainted with this jungle. So rather than give us an answer, Jesus gives us a far greater gift. He gives us himself.

Does he remove the jungle? No, the vegetation is still thick.

Does he purge the predators? No, danger still lurks.

Jesus doesn't give hope by changing the jungle; he restores our hope by giving us himself. And he has promised to stay until the very end. "I am with you always, to the very end of the age" (Matt. 28:20).

We need that reminder. We all need that reminder. For all of us need hope.

Perhaps you don't need it right now. Your jungle has become a meadow and your journey a delight. If such is the case, congratulations. But remember, we do not know what tomorrow holds. We do not know where this road will lead. You may be one turn from a cemetery, from a virus, from an empty house. You may be a bend in the road from a jungle.

And though you don't need your hope restored today, you may tomorrow. And you need to know to whom to turn.

Or perhaps you do need hope today. You know you were not made for this place. You know you are not equipped. You want someone to lead you out.

If so, put your trust in the Shepherd. He knows the path that leads to your new beginning. And he's just waiting for you to join him.

chapter two

Give Your Fears
to Your Father

I will fear no evil.
—PSALM 23:4 NKJV

It's the expression of Jesus that puzzles us. We've never before seen his face like this.

Jesus smiling, yes.

Jesus weeping, absolutely.

Jesus stern, even that.

But Jesus anguished? Cheeks streaked with tears? Face flooded in sweat? Rivulets of blood dripping from his chin? You remember the night.

Jesus left the city and went to the Mount of Olives, as he often did, and his followers went with him. When he reached the place, he said to them, "Pray for strength against temptation."

Then Jesus went about a stone's throw away from them. He kneeled down and prayed, "Father, if you are willing, take away this cup of suffering. But do what you want, not what I want." Then an angel from heaven appeared to him to strengthen him. Being full of pain, Jesus prayed even harder. His sweat was like drops of blood falling to the ground. (Luke 22:39–44 NCV)

The Bible I carried as a child contained a picture of Jesus in the Garden of Gethsemane. His face was soft, hands calmly folded as he knelt beside a rock and prayed. Jesus seemed peaceful. One reading of the Gospels disrupts that image. Mark says, "Jesus fell to the ground" (Mark 14:35 NCV). Matthew tells us Jesus was "very sad and troubled . . . to the point of death" (Matt. 26:37–38 NCV). According to Luke, Jesus was "full of pain" (Luke 22:44 NCV).

Equipped with those passages, how would you paint this scene? Jesus flat on the ground? Face in the dirt? Extended hands gripping grass? Body rising and falling with sobs? Face as twisted as the olive trees that surround him?

What do we do with this image of Jesus?

Simple. We turn to it when we look the same. We read it when we feel the same; we read it when we feel afraid. For isn't it likely that fear was one of the emotions Jesus felt? One might even argue that fear was the primary emotion. He saw something in the future so fierce, so foreboding that he begged for a change of plans. "Father, if you are willing, take away this cup of suffering" (Luke 22:42 NCV).

What causes you to pray the same prayer? Leaving your house? Being in a crowd? Walking into a hospital? Boarding an airplane? Speaking publicly? Starting a new job? Taking a spouse? Driving on a highway? The source of your fear may seem small to others. But it freezes your feet, makes your heart pound, and brings blood to your face. That's what happened to Jesus.

He was so afraid that he bled. Doctors describe this condition as hematidrosis. Severe anxiety causes the release of chemicals that break down the capillaries in the sweat glands. When this occurs, sweat comes out tinged with blood.

Jesus was more than anxious; he was afraid. Fear is worry's big brother. If worry is a burlap bag, fear is a trunk of concrete. It wouldn't budge.

How remarkable that Jesus felt such fear. But how kind that he told us about it. We tend to do the opposite. Gloss over our fears. Cover them up. Keep our sweaty palms in our pockets, our nausea and dry mouths a secret. Not so with Jesus. We see no mask of strength. But we do hear a request for strength.

"Father, if you are willing, take away this cup of suffering." The first one to hear his fear is his Father. He could have gone to his mother. He could have confided in his disciples. He could have assembled a prayer meeting. All would have been appropriate, but none were his priority. He went first to his Father.

Oh, how we tend to go everywhere else. First to the bar, to the counselor, to the self-help book, or to the friend next door. Not Jesus. The first one to hear his fear was his Father in heaven.

A millennium earlier David was urging the fear-filled to do the same. "I will fear no evil." How could David make such a claim? Because he knew where to look. "You are with me; Your rod and Your staff, they comfort me" (Ps. 23:4 NKJV)

Rather than turn to the other sheep, David turned to the Shepherd. Rather than stare at the problems, he stared at the rod and staff. Because he knew where to look, David was able to say, "I will fear no evil."

How did Jesus endure the terror of the crucifixion? He went first to the Father with his fears. He modeled the words of Psalm 56:3: "When I am afraid, I will put my trust in you" (NLT).

Do the same with yours. Don't avoid life's Gardens of Gethsemane. Enter them. Just don't enter them alone. And while there, be honest. Pounding the ground is permitted. Tears are allowed. And if you sweat blood, you won't be the first. Do what Jesus did; open your heart.

And be specific. Jesus was. "Take *this* cup," he prayed. Give God the date of the event. Provide the number of the flight. Tell him about the doctor's appointment. Share the details of the job transfer. He has plenty of time. He also has plenty of compassion.

He doesn't think your fears are foolish or silly. He won't tell you to "buck up" or "get tough." He's been where you are. He knows how you feel.

And he knows what you need. That's why we punctuate our prayers as Jesus did. "If you are willing . . ."

Was God willing? Yes and no. He didn't take away the cross, but he took the fear. God didn't still the storm, but he calmed the sailor.

Who is to say he won't do the same for you?

"Do not be anxious about anything, but in every situation, by prayer and petition, with thanksgiving, present your requests to God" (Phil. 4:6).

Don't measure the size of the mountain; talk to the One who can move it. Instead of carrying the world on your shoulders, talk to the One who holds the universe on his. Hope is a look away.

Now, what were you looking at?

chapter three

Seeing with Eyes Closed

*Faith means . . . knowing that something
is real even if we do not see it.*
—HEBREWS 11:1 NCV

When my daughters were young, I tried an experiment to teach them to see with their eyes closed. I asked Jenna, the eight-year-old, to go to one side of the den. I had Andrea, the six-year-old, stand on the other side. Three-year-old Sara and I sat on the couch in the middle and watched. Jenna's job was to close her eyes and walk. Andrea's job was to be Jenna's eyes and talk her safely across the room.

With directions like "Take two baby steps to the left" and "Take four giant steps straight ahead," Andrea successfully navigated her sister through a treacherous maze of chairs, a vacuum cleaner, and a laundry basket.

Then Jenna took her turn. She guided Andrea past her mom's favorite lamp and shouted just in time to keep her from colliding into the wall when she thought her right foot was her left foot.

After several treks through the darkness, they stopped and we processed.

"I didn't like it," Jenna complained. "It's scary going where you can't see."

"I was afraid I was going to fall," Andrea agreed. "I kept taking little steps to be safe."

I can relate, can't you? We grownups don't like the dark either. But we walk in it. We, like Jenna, often complain about how scary it is to walk where we can't see. And we, like Andrea, often take timid steps so we won't fall.

We've reason to be cautious: We are blind. We can't see the future. We have absolutely no vision beyond the present. I'm not talking near-sightedness or obstructed view; I'm talking opaque blindness. I'm not talking about a condition that passes with childhood; I'm describing a condition that passes only with death. We are blind. Blind to the future.

It's one limitation we all share. The wealthy are just as blind as the poor. The educated are just as sightless as the unschooled. And the famous know as little about the future as the unknown.

None of us know how our children will turn out. None of us know the day we will die. None of us know if another pandemic is on the way. We are universally, absolutely, unalterably blind.

We are all Jenna with her eyes shut, groping through a dark room, listening for a familiar voice—but with one difference. Her surroundings were familiar and friendly. Ours can be hostile and fatal. Her worst fear was a stubbed toe. Our worst fear is more threatening: cancer, divorce, loneliness, death.

And try as we might to walk as straight as we can, chances are a toe is going to get stubbed, and we are going to get hurt.

Just ask Jairus. He is a man who has tried to walk as straight as he could. But Jairus is a man whose path has taken a sudden turn into a cave—a dark cave. And he doesn't want to enter it alone.

Jairus is the leader of the synagogue. That may not mean much to you and me, but in the days of Christ, the leader of the synagogue was the most important man in the community. The synagogue was the center of religion, education, leadership, and social activity. The leader of the synagogue was the senior religious leader, the highest-ranking professor, the mayor, and the best-known citizen all in one.

Jairus has it all. Job security. A guaranteed welcome at the coffee shop. A pension plan. Golf every Thursday and an annual all-expenses-paid trip to the national convention.

Who could ask for more? Yet Jairus does. He *has* to ask for more. In fact, he would trade the whole package of perks and privileges for just one assurance—that his daughter will live.

The Jairus we see in this story is not the clear-sighted, black-frocked, nicely groomed civic leader. He is instead a blind man begging for a gift. He falls at Jesus' feet, "saying again and again, 'My daughter is dying. Please come and put your hands on her so she will be healed and will live'" (Mark 5:23 NCV).

He doesn't barter with Jesus. ("You do me a favor, and I'll see you are taken care of for life.") He doesn't negotiate with Jesus. ("The guys in Jerusalem are getting pretty testy about your antics. Tell you what, you handle this problem of mine, and I'll make a few calls . . .") He doesn't make excuses. ("Normally I'm not this desperate, Jesus, but I've got a problem.")

He just pleads.

There are times in life when everything you have to offer is nothing compared to what you are asking to receive. Jairus is at such a point. What could a man offer in exchange for his child's life? So there are no games. No negotiations. No masquerades. The situation is starkly simple: Jairus is blind to the future, and Jesus knows the future. So Jairus asks for his help.

And Jesus, who loves to give new beginnings, goes to give it.

And God, who knows what it is like to lose a child, empowers his Son.

But before Jesus and Jairus get very far, they are interrupted by emissaries from his house.

"Your daughter is dead. There is no need to bother the teacher anymore" (v. 35 NCV).

Get ready. Hang on to your hat. Here's where the story gets moving. Jesus goes from being led to leading, from being convinced by Jairus to convincing Jairus. From being admired to being laughed at, from helping out the people to casting out the people.

Here is where Jesus takes control.

"But Jesus paid no attention to what they said . . ." (v. 36 NCV).

I love that line! It describes the critical principle for seeing the unseen: Ignore what people say. Block them out. Turn them off. Close your ears. And, if you must, walk away.

Ignore the ones who say it's too late to begin again.

Disregard those who say you'll never amount to anything.

Turn a deaf ear toward those who say you aren't smart enough, fast enough, tall enough, or big enough—ignore them.

Faith sometimes begins by stuffing your ears with cotton.

Jesus turns immediately to Jairus and pleads: "Don't be afraid; just believe" (v. 36 NCV).

Jesus compels Jairus to see the unseen. When Jesus says, "Just believe . . . ," he is imploring, "Don't limit your possibilities to the visible.

Don't listen only for the audible. Don't be controlled by the logical. Believe there is more to life than meets the eye!"

"Trust me," Jesus is pleading. "Don't be afraid; just trust."

A father in the Bahamas cried out the same plea to his young son who was trapped in a burning house. The two-story structure was engulfed in flames, and the family—the father, mother, and several children—was on its way out when the smallest boy became terrified and ran back upstairs. His father, outside, shouted to him: "Jump, Son, jump! I'll catch you." The boy cried: "But, Daddy, I can't see you." "I know," his father called, "but I can see you."

The father could see, even though the son could not.

A similar example of faith was found on the wall of a concentration camp. On it a prisoner had carved these words:

> I believe in the sun, even though it doesn't shine,
> I believe in love, even when it isn't shown,
> I believe in God, even when he doesn't speak.

I try to imagine the person who etched those words. I try to envision the skeletal hand gripping the broken glass or stone that cut into the wall. I try to imagine eyes squinting through the darkness as each letter was carved. What hand could have cut such a conviction? What eyes could have seen good in such horror?

There is only one answer: eyes that chose to see the unseen.

As Paul wrote: "We set our eyes not on what we see but on what we cannot see. What we see will last only a short time, but what we cannot see will last forever" (2 Cor. 4:18 NCV).

Jesus is asking Jairus to see the unseen. To make a choice. Either to live by the facts or to see by faith. When tragedy strikes, we, too, are left to choose what we see. We can see either the hurt or the Healer.

The choice is ours.

Jairus makes his choice. He opts for faith and Jesus, . . . and faith *in* Jesus leads him to his daughter.

At the house Jesus and Jairus encounter a group of mourners. Jesus is troubled by their wailing. It bothers him that they express such anxiety over death. "Why are you crying and making so much noise? The child is not dead, only asleep" (Mark 5:39 NCV).

That's not a rhetorical question. It's an honest one. From Jesus' perspective the girl is not dead—she is only asleep. From God's viewpoint death is not permanent. It is a necessary step for passing from this world to the next. It's not an end; it's a beginning.

As a young boy I had two great loves—playing and eating. Summers were made for afternoons on the baseball diamond and meals at Mom's dinner table. Mom had a rule, however. Dirty, sweaty boys could never eat at the table. Her first words to us as we came home were always "Go clean up, and take off those clothes if you want to eat."

Now no boy is fond of bathing and dressing, but I never once complained and defied my mom by saying, "I'd rather stink than eat!" In my economy a bath and a clean shirt were a small price to pay for a good meal.

And from God's perspective death is a small price to pay for the privilege of sitting at his table. "Flesh and blood cannot have a part in the kingdom of God. . . . This body that can be destroyed *must* clothe itself with something that can never be destroyed. And this body that dies *must* clothe itself with something that can never die" (1 Cor. 15:50, 53 NCV, emphasis added).

God is even more insistent than my mom was. In order to sit at his table, a change of clothing *must* occur. And we must die for our body to be exchanged for a new one. So from God's viewpoint death is not to be dreaded; it is to be welcomed.

And when he sees people crying and mourning over death, he wants to know, "Why are you crying?" (Mark 5:39 NCV).

When we see death, we see disaster. When Jesus sees death, he sees deliverance.

That's too much for the people to take. "They laughed at him" (v. 40 NCV). (The next time people mock you, you might remember they mocked him too.)

Now look closely because you aren't going to believe what Jesus does next. He throws the mourners out! That's what the text says: "after throwing them out of the house . . ." (v. 40 NCV). He doesn't just ask them to leave. He *throws* them out. He picks them up by collar and belt and sends them sailing. Jesus' response is decisive and strong. In the original text the word used here is the same word used to describe what Jesus did to the money changers in the temple. It's the same verb used *thirty-eight* times to describe what Jesus did to the demons.

Why? Why such force? Why such intolerance?

Perhaps the answer is found by going back to that living-room experience with my children. After Jenna and Andrea had taken turns guiding each other through the den, I decided to add a diabolical twist. On the last trip I snuck up behind Jenna, who was walking with her eyes shut, and began whispering, "Don't listen to her. Listen to me. I'll take care of you."

Jenna stopped. She analyzed the situation and made her choice between the two voices. "Be quiet, Daddy," she giggled and then continued in Andrea's direction.

Undeterred I grabbed the lid of a pan, held it next to her ear, and banged it with a spoon. She jumped and stopped, startled by the noise. Andrea, seeing that her pilgrim was frightened, did a great thing. She ran across the room and threw her arms around her sister and said, "Don't worry. I'm right here."

She wasn't about to let the noise distract Jenna from the journey.

And God isn't going to let the noise distract you from yours. He's still busy casting out the critics and silencing the voices that could deter you.

Some of his work you have seen. Most of it you haven't. Only when you get home, will you know how many times he has protected you from disastrous decisions or a deadly illness.

Mark it down: God knows you and I are blind. He knows living by faith and not by sight doesn't come naturally. And I think that's one reason he raised Jairus's daughter from the dead. Not for her sake. She was better off in heaven. But for our sake—to teach us that heaven notices when we trust.

One final thought from the seeing-with-your-eyes-closed experiment. I asked Jenna how she could hear Andrea's voice guiding her across the room when I was trying to distract her by whispering in her ear.

Her answer? "I just concentrated and listened as hard as I could."

chapter four

Don't Give Up

*I leave the past behind and with
hands outstretched to whatever lies
ahead I go straight for the goal.*
—PHILIPPIANS 3:13–14 (PHILLIPS)

I have a distinct memory from the 1991 Super Bowl. I'm not a football junkie. Nor do I have extraordinary recall. Truth is, I don't remember anything about the '91 football season except this one detail. A headline. An observation prompted by Scott Norwood's kick.

He played for the Buffalo Bills. The city of Buffalo hadn't won a major sports championship since 1965. But that night in Tampa Bay it appeared the ball would finally bounce the Bills' way. They went back and forth with the New York Giants. With seconds to go they were a point down. They reached the Giants' twenty-nine yard line. There was time for only one more play. They turned to their kicker, Scott Norwood. All-Pro. Leading scorer of the team. As predictable as snow in Buffalo. One season he made thirty-two of thirty-seven attempts. He'd scored from this distance five times during the season. He needed to do it a sixth time.

The world watched as Norwood went through his prekick routine. He tuned out the crowd, selected a target line, got a feel for the timing, waited for the snap, and kicked the ball. He kept his head down and followed through. By the time he looked up, the ball was three-quarters of the way to the goal. That's when he realized he'd missed.

The wrong sideline erupted.

All of Buffalo groaned.

Norwood hung his head.

The headline would read "Wide and to the right: The kick that will forever haunt Scott Norwood."[1]

No do-overs. No second chance. No reprieve. He couldn't rewind the tape and create a different result. He had to live with the consequences.

So did you.

When you lost your job, flunked the exam, dropped out of school. When your marriage went south. When your business went broke. When you failed. The voices began to howl. Monkeys in a cage, they were, laughing at you. You heard them.

And you joined them! You disqualified yourself, berated yourself, upbraided yourself. You sentenced yourself to a life of hard labor in the Leavenworth of poor self-worth.

Oh, the voices of failure.

Failure finds us all. Failure is so universal we must wonder why more self-help gurus don't address it. Bookstores overflow with volumes on how to succeed. But you'll look a long time before you find a section called "How to Succeed at Failing."

Maybe no one knows what to say. But God does. His book is written for failures. It is full of folks who were foul-ups and flops but got a second chance. David was a moral failure, yet he became a man after God's own heart. Elijah was an emotional train wreck after Mount Carmel, but God used him to bring outpourings of God's grace. Jonah was in the belly of a fish when he prayed his most honest prayer and then brought revival to Nineveh.

Perfect people? No. Perfect messes? You bet. Yet God used them. A surprising and welcome discovery of the Bible is this: God uses failures.

One stumble does not define or break a person. Though you failed, God's love does not. Face your failures with faith in God's goodness. He saw this collapse coming. When you stood on the eastern side of the Jordan, God could see the upcoming mishap of your Ai.

Still, he tells you what he told Joshua: "Arise, go . . . , you and all this people, to the land which I am giving" (Josh. 1:2 NKJV). There is no condition in that covenant. No fine print. No performance language. God's promised-land offer does not depend on your perfection. It depends on his.

In God's hands no defeat is a crushing defeat. "The steps of good men are directed by the Lord. He delights in each step they take. If they fall, it isn't fatal, for the Lord holds them with his hand" (Ps. 37:23–24 TLB).

How essential it is that you understand this. Miss this truth and miss your new beginning. You must believe that God's grace is greater than your failures. Pitch your tent on promises like this one: "There is now no condemnation for those who are in Christ Jesus . . . who do not walk according to the flesh but according to the Spirit" (Rom. 8:1, 4 NASB).

Everyone stumbles. The difference is in the response. Some stumble into the pit of guilt. Others tumble into the arms of God. Those who find grace do so because they "walk according . . . to the Spirit." They hear God's voice. They make a deliberate decision to stand up and lean into God's grace.

As God told Joshua, "Do not be afraid, nor . . . dismayed; . . . *arise, go* . . ." (Josh. 8:1 NKJV, emphasis added).

The prodigal son did this. He resolved, "I will arise and go to my father" (Luke 15:18 NKJV).

Remember his story? Just like you, he was given an inheritance; he was a member of the family. Perhaps just like you, he squandered it on wild living and bad choices. He lost every penny. His trail dead-ended in a pigpen. He fed hogs for a living.

One day he was so hungry that the slop smelled like sirloin. He leaned over the trough, took a sniff, and drooled. He tied a napkin around his neck and pulled a fork out of his pocket and sprinkled salt on the slop. He was just about to dig in when something within him awoke. *Wait a second. What am I doing wallowing in the mud, rubbing shoulders with the swine?* Then he made a decision that changed his life forever. "I will arise and go to my father."

You can do that! Perhaps you can't solve all your problems or disentangle all your knots. You can't undo all the damage you've done. But you can arise and go to your Father.

Landing in a pigpen stinks. But staying there is just plain stupid.

Begin again. Rise up and step out. Fresh starts require a determined first step. Even the apostle Paul had to make this choice. "I leave the past behind and with hands outstretched to whatever lies ahead I go straight for the goal" (Phil. 3:13–14 PHILLIPS).

There ain't no future in the past. You can't change yesterday, but you can do something about tomorrow. *Put God's plan in place.*

God told Joshua to revisit the place of failure. "Arise, go up to Ai. See, I have given into your hand the king of Ai, his people, his city, and his land" (Josh. 8:1 NKJV). In essence God told Joshua, "Let's begin again. This time my way."

Joshua didn't need to be told twice. He and his men made an early morning march from Gilgal to Ai, a distance of about fifteen miles. He positioned a crack commando unit behind the town.[2] Behind this contingent was a corps of five thousand men (v. 12).

Joshua then took another company of soldiers. They headed in the direction of the city. The plan was straight out of basic military tactics. Joshua would attack, then retreat, luring the soldiers of Ai away from their village. It worked.

The king of Ai, still strutting from victory number one, set out for victory number two. He marched toward Joshua, leaving the town unprotected. The elite squad charged in and set fire to the city. And Joshua reversed his course, catching the army of Ai in the middle. The victory was complete.

Contrast this attack with the first one. In the first, Joshua consulted spies; in the second, he listened to God. In the first, he stayed home. In the second, he led the way. The first attack involved a small unit. The second involved many more men. The first attack involved no tactics. The second was strategic and sophisticated.

The point? God gave Joshua a new plan: Begin again, my way. When he followed God's strategy, victory happened.

Peter, too, discovered the wonder of God's second chance. One day Jesus used his boat as a platform. The crowd on the beach was so great that Jesus needed a buffer. So he preached from Peter's boat. Then he told Peter to take him fishing.

The apostle-to-be had no interest. He was tired; he had fished all night. He was discouraged; he had caught nothing. He was dubious. What did Jesus know about catching fish? Peter was self-conscious. People packed the beach. Who wants to fail in public?

But Jesus insisted. And Peter relented. "At Your word I will let down the net" (Luke 5:5 NKJV).

This was a moment of truth for Peter. He was saying, "I will begin again, your way." When he did, the catch of fish was so great the boat nearly sank. Sometimes we just need to begin again with Christ in the boat.

Don't spend another minute in the pigpen. It's time to rise up.

Don't miss your opportunity by inaction. It's time to step out.

God has not forgotten you. Keep your head up. You never know what good awaits you.

Scott Norwood walked off the football field with his head down. For a couple of days thoughts of the missed kick never left him. He couldn't sleep. He couldn't find peace. He was still upset when the team returned to Buffalo. In spite of the loss the city hosted an event to honor the team. The turnout was huge—between twenty-five and thirty thousand people. Norwood attended and took his place on the platform with the other players.

He attempted to linger in the background, hidden behind the others. But the fans had something else in mind. In the middle of a civic leader's speech, this chant began:

"We want Scott."

The chant grew louder.

"We want Scott!"

Scott remained behind his teammates. After all, he didn't know why the crowd wanted him.

The chant grew in volume until the speaker had to stop. Norwood's teammates pushed him to the front of the stage. When the fans saw Scott, they gave him a rousing ovation. He missed the kick, but they made sure he knew he was still a part of their community.

The Bible says that we are surrounded by a great cloud of witnesses (Heb. 12:1). Thousands upon thousands of saved saints are looking down on us. Abraham. Peter. David. Paul . . . and Joshua. Your grandma, uncle, neighbor, coach. They've seen God's great grace, and they are all pulling for you.

Press your ear against the curtain of eternity and listen. Do you hear them? They are chanting your name. They are pulling for you to keep going.

"Don't quit!"

"It's worth it!"

"Begin again!"

You may have missed a goal, but you're still a part of God's team.

chapter five

Follow the God Who Follows You

Surely goodness and mercy shall follow me
all the days of my life.
—PSALM 23:6 NKJV

Eric Hill had everything you'd need for a bright future. He was twenty-eight years old and a recent college grad with an athletic frame and a soft smile. His family loved him, girls took notice of him, and companies had contacted him about working for them. Although Eric appeared composed without, he was tormented within. Tormented by voices he could not still. Bothered by images he could not avoid. So, hoping to get away from them all, he got away from it all. On a gray, rainy day in February 1982, Eric Hill walked out the back door of his Florida home and never came back.

His sister Debbie remembers seeing him leave, his tall frame ambling down the interstate. She assumed he would return. He didn't. She hoped he would call. He didn't. She thought she could find him. She couldn't. Where Eric journeyed, only God and Eric know, and neither of them has chosen to tell. What we do know is Eric heard a voice. And in that voice was an "assignment." And that assignment was to pick up garbage along a roadside in San Antonio, Texas.

To the commuters on Interstate 10, his lanky form and bearded face became a familiar sight. He made a home out of a hole in a vacant lot. He made a wardrobe out of split trousers and a torn sweatshirt. An old hat deflected the summer sun. A plastic bag on his shoulders softened the winter chill. His weathered skin and stooped shoulders made him look twice his forty-four years. But then, sixteen years on the side of the road would do that to you.

That was how long it had been since Debbie had seen her brother. She might never have seen him again had it not been for two events. The first was the construction of a car dealership on Eric's vacant lot. The second was a severe pain in his abdomen. The dealership took his home. The pain nearly took his life.

EMS found him curled in a ball on the side of the road, clutching his stomach. The hospital ran some tests and found that Eric had cancer. Terminal cancer. Another few months and he would be dead. And with no known family or relatives, he would die alone.

His court-appointed attorney couldn't handle this thought. "Surely someone is looking for Eric," he reasoned. So the lawyer scoured the Internet for anyone in search of a brown-haired, adult male with the last name Hill. That's how he met Debbie.

His description seemed to match her memory, but she had to know for sure.

So Debbie came to Texas. She and her husband and two children rented a hotel room and set out to find Eric. By now he'd been released from the hospital, but the chaplain knew where he was. They found him sitting against a building not far from the interstate. As they approached, he stood. They offered fruit; he refused. They offered juice; he declined. He was polite but unimpressed with this family who claimed to be his own.

His interest perked, however, when Debbie offered him a pin to wear, an angel pin. He said yes. Her first time to touch her brother in sixteen years was the moment he allowed her to pin the angel on his shirt.

Debbie intended to spend a week. But a week passed, and she stayed. Her husband returned home, and she stayed. Spring became summer, and Eric improved, and still she stayed. Debbie rented an apartment and began homeschooling her kids and reaching out to her brother.

It wasn't easy. He didn't recognize her. He didn't know her. One day he cursed her. He didn't want to sleep in her apartment. He didn't want her food. He didn't want to talk. He wanted his vacant lot. He wanted his "job." Who was this woman anyway?

But Debbie didn't give up on Eric. She understood that he didn't understand. So she stayed.

I met her one Sunday when she visited our congregation. When she shared her story, I asked what you might want to ask. "How do you keep from giving up?"

"Simple," she said. "He's my brother."

I told her that her pursuit reminded me of another pursuit, that her heart reminded me of another heart. Another kind heart who left home in search of the confused. Another compassionate soul who couldn't bear the thought of a brother or sister in pain. So, like Debbie, he left home. Like Debbie, he found his sibling.

And when Jesus found us, we acted like Eric. Our limitations kept us from recognizing the One who came to save us. We even doubted his presence—and sometimes we still do.

How does he deal with our doubts? He follows us. As Debbie followed Eric, God follows us. He pursues us until we finally see him as our Father, even if it takes *all the days of our lives*.

"Surely goodness and mercy shall follow me all the days of my life; and I will dwell in the house of the LORD forever" (Ps. 23:6 NKJV).

This must be one of the sweetest phrases ever penned. Can we read it from a few other translations?

"Goodness and love unfailing, these will follow me all the days of my life, and I shall dwell in the house of the LORD my whole life long" (NEB).

"I know that your goodness and love will be with me all my life; and your house will be my home as long as I live" (GNT).

"Your beauty and love chase after me every day of my life. I'm back home in the house of GOD for the rest of my life" (THE MESSAGE).

To read the verse is to open a box of jewels. Each word sparkles and begs to be examined in the face of our doubts: *goodness, mercy, all the days, dwell in the house of the Lord, forever*. They sweep in on our insecurities like the Special Forces on a terrorist.

Look at the first word: *surely*. David didn't say, "*Maybe* goodness and mercy shall follow me." Or "*Possibly* goodness and mercy shall follow me." Or "*I have a hunch* that goodness and mercy shall follow me." David could have used one of those phrases. But he didn't. He believed in a sure God, who makes sure promises and provides a sure foundation. David would have loved the words of one of his great-great-grandsons, the apostle James. He described God as the one "with whom there is never the slightest variation or shadow of inconsistency" (James 1:17 PHILLIPS).

Our moods may shift, but God's doesn't. Our minds may change, but God's doesn't. Our devotion may falter, but God's never does. Even if we are faithless, he is faithful, for he cannot betray himself (2 Tim. 2:13). He is a sure God. And because he is a sure God, we can state confidently, "Surely goodness and mercy shall follow me all the days of my life."

And what follows the word *surely*? "Goodness and mercy." If the Lord is the shepherd who leads the flock, goodness and mercy are the two sheepdogs that guard the rear of the flock. Goodness *and* mercy. Not goodness alone, for we are sinners in need of mercy. Not mercy alone, for we are fragile, in need of goodness. We need them both. As one man wrote, "Goodness to supply every want. Mercy to forgive every sin. Goodness to provide. Mercy to pardon."[1]

Goodness and mercy—the celestial escort of God's flock. If that duo doesn't reinforce your faith, try this phrase: "all the days of my life."

What a huge statement. Look at the size of it! Goodness and mercy follow the child of God each and every day! Think of the days that lie ahead. What do you see? Days at home with only toddlers? God will be at your side. Days in a dead-end job? He will walk you through them. Days of loneliness? He will take your hand. Surely goodness and mercy shall follow me—not some, not most, not nearly all—but all the days of my life.

And what will he do during those days? He will "follow" you.

What a surprising way to describe God! We're accustomed to a God who remains in one place. A God who sits enthroned in the heavens and rules and ordains. David, however, envisions a mobile and active God. One who follows us as we begin again. Dare we do the same? Dare we envision a God who follows us? Who pursues us? Who chases us? Who tracks us down and wins us over? Who follows us with "goodness and mercy" all the days of our lives?

Isn't this the kind of God described in the Bible? A God who follows us? There are many in the Scriptures who would say so. You have to go no farther than the third chapter of the first book before you find God in the role of a seeker. Adam and Eve are hiding in the bushes, partly to cover their bodies, partly to cover their sin. But does God wait for them to come to him? No, the words ring in the garden: "Where are you?" (Gen. 3:9 NCV). With that question God began a quest for the heart of humanity that continues up to and through the moment you read these words.

Moses can tell you about it. He was forty years in the desert when he looked over his shoulder and saw a bush blazing. God had followed him into the wilderness.

Jonah can tell you about it. He was a fugitive on a boat when he looked over his shoulder and saw clouds brewing. God had followed him onto the ocean.

The disciples of Jesus knew the feeling of being followed by God. They were rain soaked and shivering when they looked over their shoulders and saw Jesus walking toward them. God had followed them into the storm.

An unnamed Samaritan woman knew the same. She was alone in life and alone at the well when she looked over her shoulder and heard a Messiah speaking. God had followed her through her pain.

John the apostle was banished on Patmos when he looked over his shoulder and saw the skies begin to open. God had followed him into his exile.

Lazarus was three days dead in a sealed tomb when he heard a voice, lifted his head, and looked over his shoulder and saw Jesus standing there. God had followed him into death.

Peter had denied his Lord and gone back to fishing when he heard his name and looked over his shoulder and saw Jesus cooking breakfast. God had followed him in spite of his failure.

God is the God who follows. I wonder . . . have you sensed him following you? We often miss him. Like Eric, we don't know our Helper when he is near. But he comes.

Through the kindness of a stranger. The majesty of a sunset. The mystery of romance. Through the question of a child or the commitment of a spouse. Through a word well spoken or a touch well timed, have you sensed his presence?

If so, then release your doubts. Set them down. Be encumbered by them no longer. You are no candidate for insecurity. You are no longer a client of timidity. You can trust God. He has given his love to you; why don't you give your doubts to him?

Not easy to trust, you say? Maybe not, but neither is it as difficult as you think. Try these ideas:

Trust your faith and not your feelings. You don't feel spiritual each day? Of course you don't. But your feelings have no impact on God's presence. On the days you don't feel close to God, trust your faith and not your feelings. Goodness and mercy shall follow you all the days of your life.

Measure your value through God's eyes, not your own. To everyone else, Eric Hill was a homeless drifter. But to Debbie, he was a brother. There are times in our lives when we are gangrels—homeless, disoriented, hard to help, and hard to love. In those seasons remember this simple fact: God loves you. He follows you. Why? Because you are family, and he will follow you all the days of your life.

See the big picture, not the small. Eric's home was taken. His health was taken. But through the tragedy, his family was returned to him. He got a second chance. It's never too late to begin again. Perhaps your home and health have been threatened as well. The immediate result might be pain. But the long-term result might be finding a Father you never knew. A Father who will follow you all the days of your life.

By the way, the last chapter in Eric Hill's life is the best one. Days before he died he recognized Debbie as his sister. And, in doing so, he discovered his home.[2]

We will as well. Like Eric, we have doubted our Helper. But like Debbie, God has followed us on our journey. Like Eric, we are quick to turn away. But like Debbie, God is slow to anger and determined to stay. Like Eric, we don't accept God's gifts. But like Debbie, God still gives them. He gives us his angels, not just pinned on a lapel, but placed on our path.

And most of all, God gives us himself. Even when we choose our hovel over his house and our trash over his grace, still he follows. Never forcing us. Never leaving us. Patiently persistent. Faithfully present. Using all of his power to convince us that he is who he is and that he can be trusted to give us new beginnings throughout our journey and in the end lead us home.

Trust your new beginning to him. Follow the God who follows you all the days of your life.

part two

Enjoy God's Good Gifts

I've been asking a few people about weariness. Seems we all have a way we can complete this sentence. *I was so tired that . . .*

I slipped while taking a shower and grabbed the water as if it could save me.

I thanked the elevator as I was walking out.

I blew on my ice cream to cool it off.

I entered my phone password on the microwave, instead of time duration, to heat up the pizza.

I thought my hand was my alarm clock. I stayed in bed ten minutes trying to turn it off.

I texted my friend, saying, "I can't talk now. I can't find my phone."

I threw my laundry in the garbage and my empty chip bag in the laundry basket.

I spent several minutes at a Stop sign waiting for it to turn green.

Groan. If only the price of fatigue were limited to goofy actions about which we later chuckle.

There is a weariness among us. A shoulder-slumping, eyelid-drooping fatigue with life. We work long hours and stand in long lines and long for a long weekend when we can finally escape the long list of jobs to do, people to impress, new gadgets to own, learn, or program.

We are weary. Weary from relationships that don't work or careers that don't satisfy or bodies that refuse to heal. Weary from too many trips to the cemetery, therapist, or happy hours that are anything but. Our shoulders slump. Our eyelids droop. We are tired. A tired people. A tired generation.

Blame it on our "reach for the moon" work ethic. The more diligent the effort, the more prosperous the reward. We saddle up the horse called "go get 'em" and do exactly that.

Blame our weariness on the Internet revolution. We are never unplugged! Texts, e-mails, and updates are only an arm's length away. Leave work at work? Not in this day and age. Messages drop like hailstorms, every day, all the time. Downtime becomes work time, crowding out what little margin we might have had.

Blame our exhaustion on a peculiar pride we have in margin-less living. We are proud of our long hours and late flights. Weariness is a badge of honor. If we aren't swamped and overworked, we almost hate to admit it.

The consequence? A society of exhaustion. People pushed and pulled in a thousand directions.

Are you among them? You don't have to be. Jesus has an invitation for you. "Come to Me, all who are weary and heavy-laden, and I will give you rest" (Matt. 11:28 NASB).

Rest. Isn't that what we need? Rest for the soul. God has plenty to offer.

The story is told about a poor man who lived in Eastern Europe in the early 1900s. Seeking a better life for himself and his family, he scraped together enough money to buy a third-class ticket on a steamship to New York City. He planned to find work and send for his family.

Having exhausted nearly all his money on the passage, he subsisted for the twelve-day journey on a wheel of hard cheese and a box of crackers. He looked longingly through the dining room window at the other passengers who ate hot, hearty, delicious meals. He would retreat into his tiny stateroom for his ration of cheese.

On the final day of the voyage, with the Statue of Liberty in sight, the man found himself standing at the railing next to one of the ship's stewards.

"I don't mean to pry," said the steward, "but why have we not seen you in the dining room?"

The traveler explained his lack of money and dependence upon crackers and cheese. The steward responded with shock, "Did you not know that three meals a day were included in your ticket? We set you a place every day, but you never came."

God has set you a place at his table. You've been given more than cheese and crackers. Avail yourself of every spiritual strength and blessing. Heaven knows, we need the help. God is here to give it.

chapter six

Accept the Gift of Himself

I had heard about you before,
but now I have seen you.
—JOB 42:5 TLB

It all happened in one day. One day he could choose his tee time at the nicest golf course in the country; the next he couldn't even be the caddie. One day he could Learjet across the country to see the heavyweight bout at the Las Vegas Mirage. The next he couldn't afford a city bus across town.

Talk about calm becoming chaos . . .

The first thing to go is his empire. The market crashes; his assets tumble. What is liquid goes dry. What has been up goes down. Stocks go flat, and Job goes broke. There he sits in his leather chair by his soon-to-be-auctioned-off mahogany desk when the phone rings with news of calamity number two: the kids were at a resort for the holidays when a storm blew in and took them with it.

Shell-shocked and dumbfounded, Job looks out the window into the sky that seems to be getting darker by the minute. He starts praying, telling God that things can't get any worse . . . and that's exactly what happens. He feels a pain in his chest that is more than last night's ravioli. The next thing he knows, he is bouncing in an ambulance with wires stuck to his chest and needles stuck in his arm.

He ends up tethered to a heart monitor in a hospital room, his only companion the beeps and alerts of medical machines.

Not, however, that Job lacks for conversation.

First there is his wife. Who could blame her for being upset after the week's calamities? Who could blame her for telling Job to curse God? But to curse God *and die*? If Job didn't already feel abandoned, you know he does the minute his wife tells him to pull the plug and be done with it.

Then there are his friends. They have the bedside manner of a drill sergeant and the compassion of a chain-saw killer. A revised version of their theology might read like this: "Boy, you must have done something really bad! We know that God is good, so if bad things are happening to you, then you have been bad. Period."

Does Job take that lying down? Not hardly.

"You are doctors who don't know what they are doing," he says. "Oh, please be quiet! That would be your highest wisdom."[1]

Translation? "Why don't you take your philosophy back to the pigpen where you learned it?"

"I'm not a bad man," Job argues. "I paid my taxes. I'm active in civic duties. I'm a major contributor to United Way and a volunteer at the hospital bazaar."

Job is, in his eyes, a good man. And a good man, he reasons, deserves a good answer.

"Your suffering is for your own good," states Elihu, a young minister fresh out of seminary who hasn't lived long enough to be cynical and hasn't hurt enough to be quiet. He paces back and forth in the hospital room with his Bible under his arm and his finger punching the air.

"God does all these things to a person—twice, even three times—to turn them back from the pit, that the light of life may shine on them."[2]

Job follows his pacing like you'd follow a tennis player, head turning from side to side. What the young man says isn't bad theology, but it isn't much comfort either. Job steadily tunes him out and slides lower and lower under the covers. His head hurts. His eyes burn. His legs ache. And he can't stomach any more hollow homilies.

Yet his question still hasn't been answered: "God, why is this happening to me?"

So God speaks.

Out of the thunder he speaks. Out of the sky he speaks. For all of us who would put ditto marks under Job's question and sign our names to it, he speaks.

- For the father who holds a rose taken off his son's coffin, he speaks.
- For the wife who holds the flag taken off her husband's casket, he speaks.
- For the couple with the barren womb and the fervent prayers, he speaks.

- For any person who has tried to see God through shattered glass, he speaks.
- For those of us who have dared to say, "If God is God, then . . . ," God speaks.

He speaks out of the storm and into the storm, for that is where Job is. That is where God is best heard.

God's voice thunders in the room. Elihu sits down. Job sits up. And the two will never be the same again.

"Who is this that obscures my plans with words without knowledge?"[3] Job doesn't respond.

"Brace yourself like a man; I will question you, and you shall answer me."[4]

"Where were you when I laid the foundations of the earth? Tell me, if you know so much."[5]

One question would have been enough for Job, but it isn't enough for God.

"Do you know how its dimensions were determined, and who did the surveying?" God asks. "What supports its foundations, and who laid its cornerstone as the morning stars sang together and all the angels shouted for joy?"[6]

Questions rush forth. They pour like sheets of rain out of the clouds. They splatter in the chambers of Job's heart with a wildness and a beauty and a terror that leave every Job who has ever lived drenched and speechless, watching the Master redefine who is who in the universe.

Have you ever once commanded the morning to appear and caused the dawn to rise in the east? Have you ever told the daylight to spread to the ends of the earth, to end the night's wickedness?[7]

46

God's questions aren't intended to teach; they are intended to stun. They aren't intended to enlighten; they are intended to awaken. They aren't intended to stir the mind; they are intended to bend the knees.

Has the location of the gates of death been revealed to you? Do you realize the extent of the earth? Tell me about it if you know! Where does the light come from, and how do you get there? Or tell me about the darkness. Where does it come from? Can you find its boundaries, or go to its source? But of course you know all this! For you were born before it was all created, and you are so very experienced![8]

Finally Job's feeble hand lifts, and God stops long enough for him to respond "I am nothing—how could I ever find the answers? I lay my hand upon my mouth in silence. I have said too much already."[9]

God's message has connected:

- Job is a peasant, telling the King how to run the kingdom.
- Job is an illiterate, telling e. e. cummings to capitalize his personal pronouns.
- Job is the batboy, telling Babe Ruth to change his batting stance.
- Job is the clay, telling the potter not to press so hard.

"I owe no one anything," God declares in the crescendo of the wind. "Everything under the heaven is mine."[10]

Job couldn't argue. God owes no one anything. No explanations. No excuses. No help. God has no debt, no outstanding balance, no favors to return. God owes no man anything.

Which makes the fact that he gave us everything even more astounding.

How you interpret this holy presentation is key. You can interpret God's hammering speech as a divine in-your-face tirade if you want. You can use the list of unanswerable questions to prove that God is harsh, cruel, and distant. You can use the book of Job as evidence that God gives us questions and no answers. But to do so, you need some scissors. To do so, you need to cut out the rest of the book of Job.

For that is not how Job heard it. All his life Job had been a good man. All his life he had believed in God. All his life he had discussed God, had notions about him, and had prayed to him.

But in the storm Job sees him!

He sees Hope. Lover. Destroyer. Giver. Taker. Dreamer. Deliverer.

Job sees the tender anger of a God whose unending love is often received with peculiar mistrust. Job stands as a blade of grass against the consuming fire of God's splendor. Job's demands melt like wax as God pulls back the curtain and heaven's light falls uneclipsed across the earth.

Job sees God.

God could turn away at this point. The gavel has been slammed; the verdict has been rendered. The Eternal Judge has spoken.

Ah, but God is not angry with Job. Firm? Yes. Direct? No doubt. Clear and convincing? Absolutely. But angry? No.

God is never irritated by the candle of an honest seeker.

If you underline any passage in the book of Job, underline this one: "I had heard about you before, but now I have seen you."[11]

Job sees God—and that is enough.

But it isn't enough for God. He will give Job a chance to begin again.

The years to come find Job once again sitting behind his mahogany desk with health restored and profits up. His lap is once again full of children and grandchildren and great-grandchildren—for four generations! A new beginning indeed.

If Job ever wonders why God doesn't bring back the children he has taken away, he doesn't ask. Maybe he doesn't ask because he knows that his children could never be happier than they are in the presence of this One he has seen so briefly.

Something tells me that Job would do it all again if that's what it would take to hear God's voice and stand in his presence. Even if God left him with his bedsores and bills, Job would do it again.

For God gave Job more than Job ever dreamed. God gave Job himself.

chapter seven

Rely On the
Holy Spirit

When you believed, you were marked in him
with a seal, the promised Holy Spirit.
—EPHESIANS 1:13

Why anyone would pester Hannah Lake is beyond me. If the sweet face of this ten-year-old doesn't destarch your shirt, her cherubic voice will. But according to her dad a grade school bully tried to stir up some trouble. Intimidation tactics, pressure—the pest tried it all. But Hannah didn't fold. And in the end it was not her dimples or tender voice but her faith that pulled her through.

The older student warned Hannah to prepare for battle. "Any day now I'm coming after you." Hannah didn't flinch or cry. She simply informed the perpetrator about the facts. "Do whatever you need to do," she explained. "But just know this: God is on my side."

Last word has it that no more threats have been made.

Elementary school bullies don't await you, but funeral homes do. Job transfers and fair-weather friends do. Challenges pockmark the pathway of your life. Where do you find energy to face them? God never promises an absence of distress on your new-beginning journey. But he does promise the assuring presence of his Holy Spirit.

At first blush a person might assume that the Holy Spirit is all about the spectacular and stupendous. We've seen the television images of sweating preachers, fainting and falling audiences, unintelligible tongue speaking, and questionable miracle working. While no one would deny the pupil-popping nature of the Holy Spirit's work (such as tongues of fire over the apostles' heads), a focus on the phenomenal might lead you to miss his quieter stabilizing work.

The Holy Spirit invisibly, yet indispensably, serves as a rudder for the ship of your soul, keeping you afloat and on track. This is no solo journey. Next time you feel as though it is, review some of the gifts the Spirit gives. For example, "you were sealed in Him with the Holy Spirit of promise, who is given as a pledge of our inheritance" (Eph. 1:13–14 NASB).

The Spirit seals you. The verb *sealed* stirs a variety of images. To protect a letter, you seal the envelope. To keep air out of a jar, you seal its mouth with a rubber-ringed lid. To keep oxygen from the wine, you seal the opening with cork and wax. To seal a deal, you might sign a contract or notarize a signature. Sealing declares ownership and secures contents.

The most famous New Testament "sealing" occurred with the tomb of Jesus. Roman soldiers rolled a rock over the entrance and "set a seal on the stone" (Matt. 27:66 NASB). Archaeologists envision two ribbons stretched in front of the entrance, glued together with hardened wax that bore the imprimatur of the Roman government—SPQR (*Senatus Populusque*

Romanus)—as if to say, "Stay away! The contents of this tomb belong to Rome." Their seal, of course, proved futile.

The seal of the Spirit, however, proves forceful. When you accepted Christ, God sealed you with the Spirit. "When you believed, you were marked in him with a seal, the promised Holy Spirit" (Eph. 1:13). When hell's interlopers come seeking to snatch you from God, the seal turns them away. He bought you, owns you, and protects you. God paid too high a price to leave you unguarded. As Paul writes later, "Remember, he has identified you as his own, guaranteeing that you will be saved on the day of redemption" (Eph. 4:30 NLT).

In his delightful book *The Dance of Hope*, my friend Bill Frey tells of a blind student named John, whom he tutored at the University of Colorado in 1951. One day Bill asked John how he had become blind. The sightless student described an accident that had happened in his teenage years. The tragedy took not just the boy's sight but also his hope. He told Bill, "I was bitter and angry with God for letting it happen, and I took my anger out on everyone around me. I felt that since I had no future, I wouldn't lift a finger on my own behalf. Let others wait on me. I shut my bedroom door and refused to come out except for meals."

His admission surprised Bill. The student he assisted displayed no bitterness or anger. He asked John to explain the change. John credited his father. Weary of the pity party and ready for his son to get on with life, he reminded the boy of the impending winter and told him to mount the storm windows. "Do the work before I get home or else," the dad insisted, slamming the door on the way out.

John reacted with anger. Muttering and cursing and groping all the way to the garage, he found the windows, stepladder, and tools and went to work. "They'll be sorry when I fall off my ladder and break my neck." But he didn't fall. Little by little he inched around the house and finished the chore.

The assignment achieved the dad's goal. John reluctantly realized he could still work and began to reconstruct his life. Years later he learned something else about that day. When he shared this detail with Bill, his blind eyes misted. "I later discovered that at no time during the day had my father ever been more than four or five feet from my side."[1]

The father had no intention of letting the boy fall.

Your Father has no intention of letting you fall, either. You can't see him, but he is present. You are "shielded by God's power" (1 Peter 1:5). He is "able to keep you from falling and to present you before his glory without fault and with unspeakable joy" (Jude v. 24 PHILLIPS).

Drink deeply from this truth. God is able to keep you from falling! Does he want you living in fear? No! Just the opposite. "The Spirit we received does not make us slaves again to fear; it makes us children of God. With that Spirit we cry out, 'Father.' And the Spirit himself joins with our spirits to say we are God's children" (Rom. 8:15–16 NCV).

What an intriguing statement. Deep within you God's Spirit confirms with your spirit that you belong to him. Beneath the vitals of the heart, God's Spirit whispers, "You are mine. I bought you and sealed you, and no one can take you." The Spirit offers an inward, comforting witness.

He is like a father who walks hand in hand with his little child. The child knows he belongs to his daddy, his small hand happily lost in the large one. He feels no uncertainty about his papa's love. But suddenly the father, moved by some impulse, swings his boy up into the air and into his arms and says, "I love you, Son." He puts a big kiss on the bubbly cheek and lowers the boy to the ground, and the two go on walking together.

Has the relationship between the two changed? On one level no. The father is no more the father than he was before the expression of love. But on a deeper level yes. The dad drenched, showered, and saturated the boy in love. God's Spirit does the same with us. "The love of God has been poured out in our hearts by the Holy Spirit who was given to us" (Rom. 5:5 NKJV). Note the preposition *of*. The Holy Spirit pours the love *of* God in our hearts, not love *for* God. God hands a bucket of love to the Spirit and instructs, "Douse their hearts."

There are moments when the Spirit enchants us with sweet rhapsody. *You belong to the Father. Signed, sealed, and soon-to-be delivered.* Been a while since you heard him whisper words of assurance? Then tell him. He's listening to you. And—get this!—he's speaking for you.

> The Spirit comes to the aid of our weakness. We do not even know how we ought to pray, but through our inarticulate groans the Spirit himself is pleading for us, and God who searches our inmost being knows what the Spirit means, because he pleads for God's own people in God's own way. (Rom. 8:26–27 NEB)

The Spirit comes to the aid of our weakness. What a sentence worthy of a highlighter. Who does not need this reminder? Weak bodies. Weak wills. Weakened resolves. We've known them all. The word *weakness* can refer to physical infirmities, as with the invalid who had been unable to walk for thirty-eight years (John 5:5), or spiritual impotence, as with the spiritually "helpless" of Romans 5:6 (NLT).

Whether we are feeble of soul or body or both, how good to know it's not up to us. "The Spirit himself is pleading for us."

Imagine: your value to God is so great that your needs top the Holy Spirit's to-do list. Did you have any idea that your needs are being described in heaven? The Holy Spirit "prays for us with groanings that cannot be expressed in words. And the Father who knows all hearts knows what the Spirit is saying, for the Spirit pleads for us believers in harmony with God's own will" (Rom. 8:26–27 NLT).

As I write, I'm thinking of a pandemic that has clouded our planet and of those people whose lives have been derailed by the virus. The COVID-19–infected man is isolated. He has no voice, no clout, and no influence.

But he has a friend. And his friend speaks on his behalf. The impoverished orphan of Russia, the distraught widow of the battlefield, the aging saint in the convalescent home—they may think they have no voice, no clout, no influence. But they have a friend—a counselor, a comforter—the blessed Spirit of God, who speaks the language of heaven in heaven. "He does our praying in and for us, making prayer out of our wordless sighs, our aching groans. He . . . keeps us present before God" (vv. 26–27 THE MESSAGE).

It's not up to you to pray your prayers. None of us pray as much as we should, but all of us pray more than we think because the Holy Spirit turns our sighs into petitions and tears into entreaties. He speaks for you and protects you. He makes sure you are heard. He makes sure you get home.

Now suppose a person never hears this, never learns about the sealing and intercession of the Spirit. This individual thinks that salvation security resides in self, not God, that prayer power depends on the person, not the Spirit. What kind of life will this person lead?

A parched and prayerless one. Fighting to stay spiritually afloat drains him. Thinking he stands alone before God discourages him. So he lives parched and prayerless.

But what about the one who believes in the work of the Spirit? Really believes. Suppose a person drinks from this fountain? Better still, suppose you do. Suppose you let the Spirit saturate you with assurance. After all, "we can't round up enough containers to hold everything God generously pours into our lives through the Holy Spirit!" (Rom. 5:5 THE MESSAGE).

Will you be different as a result? You bet your sweet Sunday you will. Your shoulders will lift as you release the buckling weight of self-salvation. Your knees will bend as you discover the buoyant power of the praying Spirit. New beginnings. Higher walk. Deeper prayers. And, most of all, a quiet confidence that comes from knowing it's not up to you. And you, like my young friend Hannah, can tell the pests of the world, "Do whatever you need to do. But just know this: God is on my side."

chapter eight

Shelter in His Protection

If you make the MOST HIGH your shelter,
no evil will conquer you.
—PSALM 91:9–10 NLT

*D*id I just see what I think I saw? I drove around the block for a second glance. The announcement, taped to a Stop-sign pole, had a home computer look to it: yellow paper and thick letters. Our neighbors, like yours, print and post all types of flyers. The presence of the announcement didn't surprise me, but the words did.

FOUND: POTBELLIED PIG

Two phone numbers followed: one to call during the day and another to call at night. I'd never seen such an announcement. Similar ones, sure.

FOUND: BLACK RETRIEVER

FOUND: PSYCHEDELIC SKATEBOARD

FOUND: GOLD BROOCH

But "Found: Potbellied Pig"? Who loses a pig? Who *owns* a pig? I know many pet owners, but pet-pig owners? Can you imagine providing daily care for a pig? Do pig owners invite dinner guests to pet the pig? Do they hang a sign on the outside gate: "Potbelly on Patrol"? Pig owners must be a special breed.

Even more so those who rescue them. The sign presupposes a curious moment. Someone spotted the pig lumbering down the sidewalk. "Poor thing. Climb in little piggy, piggy, piggy. The street is no place for a lonely sow. I'll take you home."

Suppose one appeared on your porch. Upon hearing a snort at your front door, would you open it? Not me. Golden retriever? You bet. German shepherd? Will do. Saint Bernard? Count on me for a few nights and a few neighborhood signs. But a potbellied pig? Sorry. I'd leave him on Jericho Road.

I wouldn't claim one. But God would. God did. God did when he claimed us.

We assume God cares for the purebreds of the world. The clean-nosed, tidy-living, convent-created souls of society. When God sees French poodles and Great Danes wandering the streets, he swings his door open. But what about the rest of us? We're prone to wander too. We find ourselves far from home. Do we warrant his oversight?

Psalm 91 offers a rousing yes! If you need to know the nature and size of God's lordship, nestle under the broad branches of David's poetry.

Those who live in the shelter of the Most High
  will find rest in the shadow of the Almighty.
This I declare about the LORD:
He alone is my refuge, my place of safety;
  he is my God, and I trust him.
For he will rescue you from every trap
  and protect you from deadly disease.
He will cover you with his feathers.
  He will shelter you with his wings.
  His faithful promises are your armor and protection.
Do not be afraid of the terrors of the night,
  nor the arrow that flies in the day.
Do not dread the disease that stalks in darkness,
  nor the disaster that strikes at midday.

(Ps. 91:1–6 NLT)

God offers more than the possibility of protection or the likelihood of protection on your journey. He guarantees he will guard you. Your serenity matters to heaven. God's presence encapsulates your life. Separating you from evil is God, your guardian.

During the Clinton-Lewinsky scandal special prosecutor Kenneth Starr spoke at our church. Because of the combustible days, a couple of tougher-than-two-dollar-steak US marshals monitored his every move. One walked ahead, the other behind. Between services they silently sized up all well-wishers. While Judge Starr sat in the break room, they stood at the door, the American version of Great Britain's Foot Guards. When I asked if he minded their presence, Judge Starr shrugged. "You know, their protection comforts."

So much more does God's. He sizes up every person who comes your way. As you walk, he leads. As you sleep, he patrols. "He will cover you with his feathers. He will shelter you with his wings" (v. 4 NLT).

59

The image of living beneath Shaddai's shadow reminds me of a rained-out picnic. My college friends and I barely escaped a West Texas storm before it pummeled the park where we were spending a Saturday afternoon. As we were leaving, my buddy brought the car to a sudden stop and gestured to a tender sight on the ground. A mother bird sat exposed to the rain, her wing extended over her baby who had fallen out of the nest. The fierce storm prohibited her from returning to the tree, so she covered her child until the wind passed.

From how many winds is God protecting you? His wing, at this moment, shields you. A slanderous critic heading toward your desk is interrupted by a phone call. A burglar en route to your house has a flat tire. A drunk driver runs out of gas before your car passes his. God, your guardian, protects you from

"every trap" (v. 3)
"deadly disease" (v. 3)
"the disease that stalks in darkness" (v. 6)
"the terrors of the night . . . the arrow that flies in the day" (v. 5)

One translation boldly promises: "Nothing bad will happen to you" (v. 10 NCV).

"Then why does it?" someone erupts. "Explain the pandemic. Or the death of our child." Here is where potbellied-pig thoughts surface. God protects Alaskan Malamutes and English Setters, but little runts like me? Perhaps your Rubik's Cube has a square that won't turn. If God is our guardian, why do bad things happen to us?

Have they? Have bad things *really* happened to you? You and God may have different definitions for the word *bad*. Parents and children do. Look up the word *bad* in a student dictionary, and you'll read definitions such as "pimple on nose," "Friday night all alone," or "pop quiz in geometry."

"Dad, this is really bad!" the youngster says. Dad, having been around the block a time or two, thinks differently. Pimples pass. And it won't be long before you'll treasure a quiet evening at home. Inconvenience? Yes. Misfortune? Sure. But *bad*? Save that adjective for emergency rooms and cemeteries.

What's bad to a child isn't always bad to a dad. When a five-year-old drops her ice cream cone, it is a catastrophe to her. Her father has a different perspective.

What you and I might rate as an absolute disaster, God may rate as a pimple-level problem that will pass. He views your life the way you view a movie after you've read the book. When something bad happens, you feel the air sucked out of the theater. Everyone else gasps at the crisis on the screen. Not you. Why? You've read the book. You know how the good guy gets out of the tight spot. God views your life with the same confidence. He's not only read your story . . . he wrote it. His perspective is different, and his purpose is clear.

God uses struggles to toughen our spiritual skin.

Consider it a sheer gift, friends, when tests and challenges come at you from all sides. You know that under pressure, your faith-life is forced into the open and shows its true colors. So don't try to get out of anything prematurely. Let it do its work so you become mature and well-developed, not deficient in any way. (James 1:2–4 THE MESSAGE)

One of God's cures for weak faith? A good, healthy struggle. Several years ago our family visited Colonial Williamsburg, a re-creation of eighteenth-century America in Williamsburg, Virginia. If you ever visit there, pay special attention to the work of the silversmith. The craftsman places an ingot of silver on an anvil and pounds it with a sledgehammer. Once the metal is flat enough for shaping, into the furnace it goes. The worker alternately heats and pounds the metal until it takes the shape of a tool he can use.

Heating, pounding.

Heating, pounding.

Deadlines, traffic.

Arguments, disrespect.

Loud sirens, silent phones.

Heating, pounding.

Heating, pounding.

Did you know that the *smith* in *silversmith* comes from the old English word *smite*? Silversmiths are accomplished smiters. So is God. Once the worker is satisfied with the form of his tool, he begins to planish and pumice it. Using smaller hammers and abrasive pads, he taps, rubs, and decorates. And no one stops him. No one yanks the hammer out of his hand and says, "Go easy on that silver. You've pounded enough!" No, the craftsman buffets the metal until he is finished with it. Some silversmiths, I'm told, keep polishing until they can see their face in the tool. When will God stop with you? When he sees his reflection in you. "The LORD will *perfect* that which concerns me" (Ps. 138:8 NKJV, emphasis mine). Jesus said, "My Father is always working" (John 5:17 NLT).

God guards those who turn to him. The pounding you feel does not suggest his distance but proves his nearness. Trust his sovereignty. Hasn't he earned your trust?

Has he ever spoken a word that proved to be false? Given a promise that proved to be a lie? Decades of following God led Joshua to conclude: "Not a word failed of any good thing which the LORD had spoken" (Josh. 21:45 NKJV). Look up *reliability* in heaven's dictionary and read its one-word definition: God. "If we are faithless he always remains faithful. He cannot deny his own nature" (2 Tim. 2:13 PHILLIPS).

Make a list of his mistakes. Pretty short, eh? Now make a list of the times he has forgiven you for yours. Who on earth has such a record? "The One who called you is completely dependable. If he said it, he'll do it!" (1 Thess. 5:24 THE MESSAGE).

You can depend on him. He is "the same yesterday and today and forever" (Heb. 13:8 ESV). And because he is the Lord, "He will be the stability of your times" (Isa. 33:6 NASB).

Trust him. "But when I am afraid, I will put my trust in you" (Ps. 56:3 NLT). Join with Isaiah, who resolved, "I will trust in him and not be afraid" (Isa. 12:2 NLT).

God is directing your steps and delighting in every detail of your life (Ps. 37:23–24 NLT). Doesn't matter who you are. Potbellied pig or prized purebred? God sees no difference. But he does see you. In fact, that's his car pulling over to the side of the road. That's God opening the door. And that's you climbing into the passenger seat to begin to see how he will write the next chapter in your story.

chapter nine

Settle Down Deep in His Love

May you experience the love of Christ,
though it is too great to understand fully.
—EPHESIANS 3:19 NLT

Pipín Ferreras wants to go deep, deeper than any person has ever gone. You and I are content with 10 or 20 feet of water. Certain risktakers descend 40, maybe 50. Not Pipín. This legendary Cuban diver has descended into 531 feet of ocean water, armed with nothing but flippers, a wet suit, deep resolve, and one breath of air.

His round trip lasted three minutes and twelve seconds. To prepare for such a dive, he loads his lungs with 8.2 liters of air—nearly twice the capacity of a normal human being—inhaling and exhaling for several minutes, his windpipe sounding like a bicycle pump. He then wraps his knees around the crossbar of an aluminum sled that lowers him to the sea bottom.[1]

No free diver has gone farther. Still, he wants more. Though he's acquainted with water pressure that tested World War II submarines, it's not enough. The mystery of the deep calls him. He wants to go deeper.

Could I interest you in a similar ear-popping descent? Not into the waters of the ocean, but into the limitless love of God.

> May your roots go down deep into the soil of God's marvelous love; and may you be able to feel and understand, as all God's children should, how long, how wide, how deep, and how high his love really is; and to experience this love for yourselves, though it is so great that you will never see the end of it or fully know or understand it. And so at last you will be filled up with God himself. (Eph. 3:17–19 TLB)

When Paul wants to describe the love of God, he can't avoid the word *deep*. Dig "deep into the soil of God's marvelous love" (v. 17). Discover "how deep . . . his love really is" (v. 18).

Envision Ferreras deep beneath the ocean surface. Having plunged the equivalent of five stories, where can he turn and not see water? To the right, to the left, beneath him, above him—the common consistency of his world is water. Water defines his dives, dictates his direction, liberates him, limits him. His world is water.

Can a person go equally deep into God's love? Sink so deep that he or she sees nothing but? David Brainerd, the eighteenth-century missionary to American Indians, would say so. He journaled:

> I withdrew to my usual place of retirement, in great tranquility. I knew only to breathe out my desire for a perfect conformity to Him in all

things. God was so precious that the world with all its enjoyments seemed infinitely vile. I had no more desire for the favor of men than for pebbles.

At noon I had the most ardent longings after God which I ever felt in my life.

In my secret retirement, I could do nothing but tell my dear Lord in a sweet calmness that He knew I desired nothing but Him, nothing but holiness, that He had given me these desires and He only could give the thing desired.

I never seemed to be so unhinged from myself, and to be so wholly devoted to God.

My heart was swallowed up in God most of the day.[2]

You will need a descent into such love on your new beginning journey. Scripture offers an anchor. Grab hold of this verse and let it lower you down: "God is love" (1 John 4:16 NLT).

One word into the passage reveals the supreme surprise of God's love—it has nothing to do with you. Others love you because of you, because your dimples dip when you smile or your rhetoric charms when you flirt. Some people love you because of you. Not God. He loves you because he is he. He loves you because he decides to. Self-generated, uncaused, and spontaneous, his constant-level love depends on his choice to give it. "The LORD did not set his affection on you and choose you because you were more numerous than other peoples, for you were the fewest of all peoples. But it was because the LORD loved you" (Deut. 7:7–8).

You don't influence God's love. You can't impact the treeness of a tree, the skyness of the sky, or the rockness of a rock. Nor can you affect the love of God. If you could, John would have used more ink: "God is *occasional* love" or "*sporadic* love" or "*fair-weather* love." If your actions altered his devotion, then God would not be love; indeed, he would be human, for this is human love.

And you've had enough of human love. Haven't you? Enough guys wooing you with Elvis-impersonator sincerity. Enough tabloids telling you that true love is just a diet away. Enough helium-filled expectations of bosses and parents and pastors. Enough mornings smelling like the mistakes you made while searching for love the night before.

Don't you need a fountain of love that won't run dry? You'll find one on a stone-cropped hill outside Jerusalem's walls where Jesus hangs, cross nailed and thorn crowned. When you feel unloved, ascend this mount. Meditate long and hard on heaven's love for you. Both eyes beaten shut, shoulders as raw as ground beef, lips bloody and split. Fists of hair yanked from his beard. Gasps of air escaping his lungs. As you peer into the crimsoned face of heaven's only Son, remember this: "God showed his great love for us by sending Christ to die for us while we were still sinners" (Rom. 5:8 NLT).

Don't trust other yardsticks. We often do. The sight of the healthy or successful prompts us to conclude, *God must really love him. He's so blessed with health, money, good looks, and skill.*

Or we gravitate to the other extreme. Lonely and frail in the hospital bed, we deduce, *God does not love me. How could he? Look at me.*

Rebuff such thoughts! Success signals God's love no more than struggles indicate the lack of it. The definitive, God-sanctioned gauge is not a good day or a bad break but the dying hours of his Son. Consider them often. Let the gap between trips to the cross diminish daily. Discover what Brainerd meant when he said, "My heart was swallowed up in God most of the day." Accept this invitation of Jesus: "Abide in My love" (John 15:9 NASB).

When you abide somewhere, you live there. You grow familiar with the surroundings. You don't pull in the driveway and ask, "Where is the garage?" You don't consult the blueprint to find the kitchen. To abide is to be at home.

To abide in Christ's love is to make his love your home. Not a roadside park or hotel room you occasionally visit, but your preferred dwelling. You rest in him. Eat in him. When thunder claps, you step beneath his roof. His walls secure you from the winds. His fireplace warms you from the winters of life. As John urged, "We take up permanent residence in a life of love" (1 John 4:17 THE MESSAGE). You abandon the old house of false love and move into his home of real love.

Adapting to this new home takes time. First few nights in a new home you can wake up and walk into a wall. I did. Not in a new home, but in a motel. Climbed out of bed to get a glass of water, turned left, and flattened my nose. The dimensions to the room were different.

The dimensions of God's love are different too. You've lived a life in a house of imperfect love. You think God is going to cut you as the coach did, or abandon you as your father did, or judge you as false religion did, or curse you as your friend did. He won't, but it takes time to be convinced.

For that reason abide in him. Hang on to Christ the same way a branch clutches the vine. According to Jesus the branch models his definition of *abiding*. "As the branch cannot bear fruit of itself unless it abides in the vine, so neither can you unless you abide in Me" (John 15:4 NASB).

Does a branch ever release the vine? Only at the risk of death. Does the branch ever stop eating? Nope. It receives nutrients twenty-four hours a day. Would you say the branch is vine dependent? I would. If branches had seminars, the topic would be "Get a Grip: Secrets of Vine Grabbing." But branches don't have seminars because attendance requires releasing the vine, something they refuse to do.

How well do you pass the vine test? Do you ever release yourself from Christ's love? Go unnourished? Do you ever stop drinking from his reservoir? Do so at the certain risk of a parched heart. Do so and expect a roundworm existence.

By sealing itself off against the world, the roundworm can endure extended seasons of drought. It essentially shuts down all systems. Releasing water until it's as dry as a cotton ball, the roundworm enters a state known as anhydrobiosis, meaning "life without water." A quarter of its body weight is converted to a material that encircles and protects its inner organs. It then shrinks to about 7 percent of its normal size and waits out the dry spell.[3]

Scientists assure us that humans can't do this. I'm not so sure.

- My friend's wife left him. "Now that the kids are grown," she announced, "it's my time to have fun."
- Recent headlines told of a man who murdered his estranged wife and kids. His justification? If he can't have them, no one will.
- Yesterday's e-mail came from a good man with a persistent porn problem. He's not convinced that God can forgive him.

Anhydrobiosis of the heart. Withdrawn emotions. Callous souls. Coiled and recoiled against the love drought of life. Hard-shelled to survive the harsh desert. We were not made to live this way. What can we do?

From the file entitled "It Ain't Gonna Happen," I pull and pose this suggestion. Let's make Christ's command a federal law. Everyone has to make God's love his or her home. Let it herewith be stated and hereby declared:

No person may walk out into the world to begin the day until he or she has stood beneath the cross to receive God's love.

Cabbies. Presidents. Preachers. Tooth pullers and truck drivers. All required to linger at the fountain of his favor until all thirst is gone. I mean a can't-drink-another-drop satisfaction. All hearts hydrous. Then, and only then, are they permitted to enter the interstates, biology labs, classrooms, and boardrooms of the world.

Don't you ache for the change we'd see? Less honking and locking horns, more hugging and helping kids. We'd pass fewer judgments and more compliments. Forgiveness would skyrocket. How could you refuse to give someone a second chance when God has made your life one big new beginning? Doctors would replace sedative prescriptions with Scripture meditation: "Six times an hour reflect on God's promise: '*I have loved you with an everlasting love*'" (Jer. 31:3 NASB; emphasis mine). And can't you hear the newscast? "Since the implementation of the love law, divorce rates have dropped, cases of runaway children have plummeted, and Republicans and Democrats have disbanded their parties and decided to work together."

Wild idea? I agree. God's love can't be legislated, but it can be chosen. Choose it, won't you? For the sake of your fresh start. For the sake of your journey. For Christ's sake, and yours, choose it. The prayer is as powerful as it is simple: "Lord, I receive your love. Nothing can separate me from your love."

My friend Keith took his wife, Sarah, to Cozumel, Mexico, to celebrate their anniversary. Sarah loves to snorkel. Give her fins, a mask, and a breathing tube, and watch her go deep. Down she swims, searching for the mysteries below.

Keith's idea of snorkeling includes fins, a mask, and a breathing tube, but it also includes a bellyboard. The surface satisfies him.

Sarah, however, convinced him to take the plunge. Forty feet offshore, she shouted for him to paddle out. He did. The two plunged into the water where she showed him a twenty-foot-tall submerged cross. "If I'd had another breath," he confessed, "the sight would have taken it away."

Jesus beckons you to descend and see the same. Forget surface glances.

No more sunburned back. Go deep. Take a breath and descend so deeply into his love that you see nothing else.

Join the psalmist in saying:

> Whom have I in heaven but you?
>> And earth has nothing I desire besides you.
>
> My flesh and my heart may fail,
>> but God is the strength of my heart
>>
>> and my portion forever. . . .
>
> My heart has heard you say, "Come and talk with me, O my people."
>> And my heart responds "Lord, I am coming." (Ps. 73:25–26 NIV;
>>
>> 27:8 TLB)

part three

Ground Yourself in His Promises

No one told me the night they changed the gas pumps. Maybe I slept through the news. Perhaps I didn't read the paper. Who knows what happened. All I know is this: I didn't know how to gas up my car. I entered the convenience store and asked the clerk for twenty dollars' worth of fuel on pump number three. But she wouldn't take my money.

"You don't have to give me money anymore."

"Are you serious?"

"Use your credit card to pay at the pump."

"Pay at the pump?"

"Pay at the pump."

Some of you are too young to know this, but we used to pay for gasoline inside the store. Yes! Ask your grandparents. Life hasn't always been this easy. When we were young, we braved the freezing cold weather or blazing heat and made the walk from pump to store. I think it was a five-mile hike. Uphill. Into the wind.

It was a great day when credit card readers were installed at the pump.

My first experience with one was confusing, however. Returning to the vehicle, I tried to figure out what to do. Hours passed. Standing between gas pump and gasless car, credit card in one hand, hose in the other, staring at the dotted letters charioting their way across the tiny screen, not believing what they were telling me to do.

"Swipe card."

Swipe card? Why swipe a card? I already have one, thank you. Besides, theft is illegal. I'm a minister. I can't go around swiping people's credit cards. But, then again, what choice did I have? I noticed a rough-looking, refrigerator-sized fellow gassing up a truck next to me. He might know something about swiping. "Hey, where do you go to swipe a credit card?"

"There," he pointed to the pump. "Right in front of your nose."

That's when I realized *swipe* meant *slide*. Not only did they change the system, they changed the language. So I complied. Even though my dad had pledged to punish me if I ever swiped anything, I did. I swiped my card through the slot. Didn't work. According to the gremlin who lives inside the pump, I swiped my card in the wrong direction. The letters said, "Swipe again."

I did but failed. Never was a good swiper.

"Look at the picture," Mr. Big Guy shouted. "You've got to swipe the stripe." Sure enough, the picture portrayed the proper stripe placement. I complied. But a good swipe wasn't enough. "Enter pin number." Pin number? Fortunately I had a pen in my pocket. Unfortunately it had no number. By now the man was gone, and all I could do was sigh.

What a position in which to be. My tank out of gas. The pump full of gas. But the connection between the pump and the car? It wasn't happening.

Do you know the feeling? I know you do. Not with your car and gas but with your heart and God's strength. You need fuel. Doesn't take long to burn up a tank. Boss demands more hours, doctor requires more tests, spouse wants more attention, church needs more volunteers—everyone wants more. Before long you are out of gas. Heaven has an ample supply of energy. But how do you make the connection? How do you put God's gas in your tank?

Here is my suggestion. Fill your tank with the promises of God. One student of Scripture spent a year and a half attempting to tally the number of promises God has made to humanity. He came up with 7,487 promises![1] God's promises are pine trees in the Rocky Mountains of Scripture: abundant, unbending, and perennial. In the next few pages let's explore some wonderful God-guarantees. You'll go further on a full tank of his love.

You'll be glad to know I finally gassed up the car. And I didn't have to swipe anything to do it.

chapter ten

Hold On to Your Soul Anchor

*We have this hope as an anchor for
the soul, firm and secure.*
—HEBREWS 6:19

Long after the kids are bathed and put to bed, the single mom
stares at the bills and checkbook balance. Too many of the first,
not much in the second. She's called on all her friends. She's
cashed in all her favors. There aren't enough hours in the day to earn more
money. She stares out the window of the small apartment and wonders
where to turn.

Then there is the weary man in the ICU standing at the bedside of his only love. He can scarcely remember a day without her. They married so young. He has never known anything as pure as this woman's heart. He leans over her face and strokes her white hair. No response. The doctor has told him to say goodbye. The husband is all out of hope.

And what about the executive who sits behind the big desk in the corner office? His handshake is firm; his voice sounds confident. But don't let his demeanor fool you. If solvency were a jet, his is in a tailspin. His banker wants to meet. His accountant wants to quit. And hope? Hope boarded a train for the coast and hasn't been seen for a week.

You know the feeling. We all do. Even the cup-is-half-full, sanguine souls who use the lyric "the sun will come out tomorrow" as their cellphone ring. Sometimes we just run out of hope. When we do, where can we turn?

I suggest we turn to this great and precious promise: "We have this hope as an anchor for the soul, firm and secure. It enters the inner sanctuary behind the curtain, where our forerunner, Jesus, has entered on our behalf" (Heb. 6:19–20).

Look at the key terms of the first phrase: *anchor* and *soul*.

You don't need to be told what an anchor is. You've held those iron castings with the pointed edges. Perhaps you've thrown one from a boat into the water and felt the yank as the tool found its lodging place. The anchor has one purpose—to steady the boat. To weather a blast of bad weather, you need a good anchor. You need one like the tattoo on Popeye's forearm—strong and double pointed. You need one that can hook securely to an object that is stronger than the storm. You need a good anchor.

Why? Because you have a valuable vessel. You have a soul. When God breathed into Adam, he gave him more than oxygen; he gave him a soul. He made him an eternal being.

Because of your soul, you wonder why you are here. Because of your soul, you wonder where you are going. Because of your soul, you wrestle with right and wrong, you value the lives of others, and you get choked up at the singing of the national anthem and teary-eyed at the sight of your baby.

Your soul unites you to God. And your soul needs an anchor. Your soul is fragile. It feels the pain of death and knows the questions of disease. Your liver may suffer from the tumor, but your soul suffers from the questions. Hence, your soul needs an anchor, a hooking point that is sturdier than the storm.

This anchor is set, not on a boat or person or possession. No, this anchor is set in "the inner sanctuary behind the curtain, where our forerunner, Jesus, has entered on our behalf" (vv. 19–20). Our anchor, in other words, is set in the very throne room of God. We might imagine the anchor attached to the throne itself. It will never break free. The rope will never snap. The anchor is set, and the rope is strong. Why? Because it is beyond the reach of the devil and under the care of Christ. Since no one can take your Christ, no one can take your hope.

Do critics define your identity? No, because God said, "Let us make human beings in our image" (Gen. 1:26 NCV). That includes you.

Can challenges deplete your strength? No, because "we are heirs—heirs of God and co-heirs with Christ" (Rom. 8:17). You have access to the family fortune.

Are you a victim of circumstances? Not in the least. "When a believing person prays, great things happen" (James 5:16 NCV).

Does God have a place for the small people of the world? You bet he does. "God resists the proud, but gives grace to the humble" (1 Peter 5:5 NKJV).

Can anyone understand what it is like to lead your life? Jesus can. "Our high priest is able to understand our weaknesses" (Heb. 4:15 NCV).

Do you feel all alone with your problems? You aren't. Jesus "is at the right hand of God and is also interceding for us" (Rom. 8:34).

Can God ever forgive your failures? He already has. "There is now no condemnation for those who are in Christ Jesus" (Rom. 8:1).

Is the grave a dead end? Just the opposite. "Death has been swallowed up in victory" (1 Cor. 15:54).

Will the sorrow ever end? Sometimes it feels as if it won't. But God has assured us: "Weeping may last through the night, but joy comes with the morning" (Ps. 30:5 NLT).

Will you have the wisdom and energy for the remainder of your life? No, you won't. But the Holy Spirit does. "You will receive power when the Holy Spirit comes on you" (Acts 1:8).

Life isn't fair! But it will be, "For [God] has set a day when he will judge the world" (Acts 17:31).

Death, failure, betrayal, sickness, disappointment—they cannot take your hope, because they cannot take your Jesus. You may believe this but still ask, "Is there any hope?" when you find yourself overwhelmed by tough times.

Are you asking that question? Are you the single mom who has no resources? The man in the ICU with no strength? The businessman with no answers? Are you asking the question, Is there any hope?

Jonathan McComb did.

The McCombs were the picture of the all-American family. Two young, beautiful children. Terrific marriage. Jonathan worked ranches. Laura sold pharmaceuticals. They were God fearing, happy, busy, and carefree. Then came the storm. Rain was in the forecast. But a once-in-a-century flood? No one saw it coming. The Blanco River rose twenty-eight feet in ninety minutes and roared through the South Texas hill country, taking homes, cars, and bridges with it. Jonathan and his family sought safety on the second floor of the cabin in which they were staying, but safety was nowhere to be found. The house was yanked off its foundation. They found themselves clutching a mattress, riding white water.

Jonathan survived.

No one else did.

When Denalyn and I visited him in the hospital, he could hardly move from the pain. But the broken ribs and hip were nothing compared to the broken heart. Jonathan tried to talk. But he mustered only tears.

A couple of weeks later he found the strength to speak at the funeral for his wife and two children. It seemed the entire city of Corpus Christi, Texas, was present. The church had no empty seats or dry eyes. For well more than half an hour, Jonathan described his wife and children. He spoke of their laughter and joy and how empty his house had become.

Then he said:

> People have been asking me how I am doing and how I can stay so strong and positive in a time like this. I have told them that I have been lean-ing on my family, my friends, and most importantly my faith. . . . After church every Sunday, Laura would always ask, "How do we get more people to come to church and learn about salvation?" Well, Laura, what do you think? They're here.
>
> A particular verse that I have loved over the years has also helped me along. "Trust in the LORD with all your heart and lean not on your own understanding" (Prov. 3:5). I have no explanation for why such a tragic event like the flood takes place and lives are lost, but I know that God is not going to give us anything we can't handle. I know that we are here for a little while, but trust me—if I could have every bone broken in my body to have them back, I would do it, but it is not our call. . . . Yes, I know that this entire tragedy is horrible, and I have been angry, upset, confused, and left to wonder why. I have cried enough tears to fill that river up a

hundred times. But I know that I can't stay angry or upset or confused or continue to ask myself why, because I will find out that answer when my time comes and I am reunited with them in heaven. But trust me, that will be the first question I ask.

I took note of the number of times Jonathan used the phrase "I know."

I know that God is not going to give us anything we can't handle.
I know that we are here for a little while . . .
I know that this entire tragedy is horrible.
I know . . . I will [be] reunited with them in heaven.

Jonathan was not naive or dismissive. He didn't react with superficial, shallow belief. He knew the tragedy was horrible. But in the midst of the storm, he found hope, an unshakable hope. He found no easy answers, but he found the Answer. He made the deliberate decision to build his life on God's promise to restore and renew.

Jesus encouraged his followers to "always pray and never lose hope" (Luke 18:1 ncv).

Never lose hope? Never be fainthearted? Never feel overwhelmed? Never get sucked into the sewer of despair? Can you imagine? No day lost to anguish. No decision driven by fear. This is God's will for you and me. He wants us to "abound in hope by the power of the Holy Spirit" (Rom. 15:13 nkjv).

Abound. What an extraordinary verb to use with "hope."

For about half an hour last week, the sky became a waterfall. I had to pull my car off the road. Windshield wipers stood no chance against the downpour. Every square inch of the highway was drenched. Rain *abounded.* God will drench your world with hope.

I once spent a day in Yosemite forest. I could no more number the trees than I could count the stars. Tall ones, small ones. To the right and left. Behind me, before me. Yosemite *abounded* in trees. God will turn your world into a forest of hope.

I remember, as a child, walking through a cotton field near my grandparents' home in West Texas. The farm *abounded* in cotton. I saw no end to it. North, south, east, west: puffy white balls on all sides. God will grant you a summer harvest of hope.

Could you use some abounding hope? Not occasional hope or sporadic hope or thermostatic hope, but abounding hope?

It's yours for the asking. "Grab the promised hope with both hands and never let go. It's an unbreakable spiritual lifeline, reaching past all appearances right to the very presence of God where Jesus, running on ahead of us, has taken up his permanent post as high priest for us" (Heb. 6:18–20 THE MESSAGE).

Ask yourself this key question: Is what I'm hooked to stronger than what I'll go through?

Everyone is anchored to something. A retirement account or a résumé. Some are tethered to a person; others are attached to a position. Yet these are surface objects. Would you anchor your boat to another boat? Heaven forbid. You want something that goes deeper and holds firmer than other floating vessels. But when you anchor to the things of this world, are you not doing the same? Can a retirement account survive a depression? Can good health weather a disease? There is no guarantee.

Salty sailors would urge you to hook on to something hidden and solid. Don't trust the buoy on the water, don't trust the sailors in the next boat, and don't trust the other boat. In fact, don't even trust your own boat. When the storm hits, trust no one but God. The apostle Paul proclaimed it triumphantly: "we have put our hope in the living God" (1 Tim. 4:10).

People of the new beginning make daily decisions to secure their anchors in the promises of God. And while you are on your journey, I urge you to create a personal book of promises, one you and God can write together. Search and search until you find covenants that address your needs. Clutch them as the precious pearls they are; hide them in your heart so they can pay dividends long into the future. When the Enemy comes with his lies of doubt and fear, you can produce the pearl. Satan will be quickly silenced. He has no reply for truth.

They work, friend. The promises of God work. They can walk you through horrific tragedies. They can buoy you in the day-to-day difficulties. They are, indeed, the great and precious promises of God.

Russell Kelso Carter learned this truth. He was a gifted athlete and student. In 1864 at the age of fifteen, during a prayer meeting he surrendered his life to Christ. He became an instructor at the Pennsylvania Military Academy in 1869. He led a diverse and fruitful life that included stints as a minister, medical doctor, and even a songwriter. But it was his understanding of God's promises that makes his story relevant to us.

By age thirty Carter had a critical heart condition and was on the brink of death. "Connie Ruth Christiansen writes: 'He knelt and made a promise that healing or no, his life was finally and forever, consecrated to the service of the Lord.' Christiansen goes on to say that from that moment on the Scripture took on new life for Carter and he began to lean on the promises that he found in the Bible. He committed himself to believe, whether or not God granted him healing. . . . Carter lived, with a healthy heart, for another 49 years."[1] His decision to trust God in the midst of difficulties gave birth to a hymn that is still sung today.

> Standing on the promises of Christ my King,
> Through eternal ages let His praises ring,
> Glory in the highest, I will shout and sing,
> Standing on the promises of God.

Refrain:

Standing, standing,

Standing on the promises of God my Savior;

Standing, standing,

I'm standing on the promises of God.

My favorite stanza is the second verse:

Standing on the promises that cannot fail,

When the howling storms of doubt and fear assail,

By the living Word of God I shall prevail,

Standing on the promises of God.[2]

Do the same.

Build your life on the promises of God. Since his promises are unbreakable, your hope will be unshakable. The winds will still blow. The rain will still fall. But in the end of your journey, you will be standing— standing on the promises of God.

chapter eleven

Choose Faith

He who promised is faithful.
—HEBREWS 10:23

I was comfortably seated in the exit row of the plane when a passenger coming down the aisle called my name. He was a tall, light-haired fellow who appeared to be about fifty years old and on a business trip. He introduced himself. Because of the chaos of boarding a flight, we couldn't chat. But this much I gathered. He had heard me speak some years earlier, had appreciated my books, and would love to talk someday.

I returned the greeting and settled in for the trip. About an hour later I felt a tap on my shoulder. I turned. It was the fellow who had greeted me in the aisle. He'd scribbled a message on a napkin and handed it to me.

Max,

Six summers ago Lynne and I buried our twenty-four-year-old daughter. This came about following a lake accident and two weeks on life support. We didn't see this coming. How do you go on a summer vacation with four and come back home with three?

Friends, some of whom had buried precious children, rallied around our family. A country lawyer with his encouraging message that "God means you good, not harm" was one of those encouraging voices. Several of your books were given to Lynne and me . . .

We prayed for a miracle. I wanted her made new, her smile and brilliance restored. To unplug our daughter from life support was very, very hard. Although the decision was painful, we were confident that we were doing the right thing in laying her in the arms of a mighty God. He knew our pain.

His best work may not have been restoring Erin to this life but his assistance for Lynne and me to let him have her. He made our daughter better than new. He restored my Erin to his eternal presence. That is his best work!

This was not a lightweight hope. This was an assurance: "Let me have your Erin. I've got her now."

God's children reflecting the very nature of God became his presence around us. Our faith is getting us through this.

Faith is a choice.[1]

I read the napkin testimony several times. I wanted to know, How does this happen? How does a dad bury a daughter and believe, so deeply believe, that God meant him good not harm, that God had received his daughter in his loving arms, that God did his best work in the hearts of sorrow? The napkin could have easily borne a different message. One of anger and bitterness. One of disappointment and despair. One full of hurt, even hate, toward God. What made this message different?

Simple. This grieving dad believes God's promises. "Faith is a choice," he concluded.

It is.

Our God is a promise-keeping God. Others may make a promise and forget it. But if God makes a promise, he keeps it. "He who promised is faithful" (Heb. 10:23).

Does this matter? Does God's integrity make a difference? Does his faithfulness come into play? When your daughter is on life support, it does. When you're pacing the ER floor, it does.

When you are wondering what to do with every parent's worst nightmare, you have to choose. Faith or fear, God's purpose or random history, a God who knows and cares or a God who isn't there? We all choose.

New-beginning people choose to trust God's promises. They choose to believe that God is up to something good even though all we see looks bad. They echo the verse of the hymn:

His oath, His covenant, His blood,
Support me in the whelming flood.[2]

Nothing deserves your attention more than God's covenants. No words written on paper will ever sustain you like the promises of God. Do you know them?

To the bereaved: "Weeping may stay for the night, but rejoicing comes in the morning" (Ps. 30:5).

To the besieged: "The righteous person may have many troubles, but the LORD delivers him from them all" (Ps. 34:19).

To the sick: "The LORD sustains them on their sickbed and restores them from their bed of illness" (Ps. 41:3).

To the lonely: "When you pass through the waters, I will be with you" (Isa. 43:2).

To the dying: "In my Father's house are many rooms. . . . I go to prepare a place for you" (John 14:2 ESV).

To the sinner: "My grace is sufficient for you" (2 Cor. 12:9).

These promises are for your good. "And because of his glory and excellence, he has given us great and precious promises. These are the promises that enable you to share his divine nature and escape the world's corruption caused by human desires" (2 Peter 1:4 NLT).

Press into God's promises. When fears surface, respond with this thought: *But God said* . . . When doubts arise, *But God said* . . . When guilt overwhelms you, *But God said* . . .

Declare these words: "You have rescued me, O God who keeps his promises" (Ps. 31:5 TLB). Turn again and again to God's spoken covenants. Search the Scriptures the way a miner digs for gold. Once you find a nugget, grasp it. Trust it. Take it to the bank. Do what I did with the promise of the pilot.

Not long after I met the note-giving gentleman on the plane, I took another flight. On this occasion a note did not come my way, but bad weather did. The flight into Houston was delayed by storms. We landed at the exact time the final flight into San Antonio was scheduled to depart. As we taxied toward the gate, I was checking my watch, thinking about hotels, preparing to call and tell Denalyn of my delay, grumbling at the bad break.

Then over the loud speaker a promise. "This is the pilot. I know many of you have connections. Relax. You'll make them. We are holding your planes. We have a place for you."

Well, I thought, *he wouldn't say that if he didn't mean it.* So I decided to trust his promise.

I didn't call Denalyn.

I stopped thinking about hotels.

I quit checking my watch.

I relaxed. I waited my turn to get off the plane and set my sights on my gate. I marched through the concourse with confidence. Hadn't the pilot given me a promise?

Other people in the airport weren't so fortunate. They, also victims of inclement weather, were in a panic. Travelers were scrambling, white faced and worried. Their expressions betrayed their fear.

Too bad their pilot hadn't spoken to them. Or perhaps he had and they hadn't listened.

Your Pilot has spoken to you. Will you listen? No, I mean *really* listen? Let his promises settle over you like the warmth of a summer day. When everyone and everything around you says to panic, choose the path of peace. In this world of empty words and broken promises, do yourself a favor: take hold of the promises of God.

My friend Wes did. You'll look a long time before you'll find a better man than Wes Bishop. He had a quick smile, warm handshake, and serious weakness for ice cream. For more than thirty-five years he kept the same job, loved the same wife, served the same church, and lived in the same house. He was a pillar in the small Texas town of Sweetwater. He raised three great sons, one of whom married my daughter Jenna. Wes never even missed a day of work until a few months ago when he was diagnosed with brain cancer.

We asked God to remove it. For a time it appeared that he had. But then the symptoms returned with a vengeance. In a matter of a few weeks, Wes was immobilized, at home, in hospice care.

The sons took turns keeping vigil so their mom could rest. They placed a baby monitor next to Wes's bed. Though he'd hardly spoken a word in days, they wanted to hear him if he called out.

One night he did. But he didn't call for help; he called for Christ. About one o'clock in the morning, the youngest son heard the strong voice of his father on the monitor. "Jesus, I want to thank you for my life. You have been good to me. And I want you to know, when you are ready to take me, I am ready to go." As it turned out, those were the final words Wes spoke. Within a couple of days Jesus took him home to heaven to start a new beginning that will last for eternity.

I want that kind of faith. Don't you? The faith that turns to God in the darkest hour, praises God with the weakest body. The kind of faith that trusts in God's promises. The kind of faith that presses an ink pen into an airline napkin and declares, "Faith is a choice. And I choose faith."

chapter twelve

Let Your Father Fight for You

With us is the LORD our God, to help
us and to fight our battles.
—2 CHRONICLES 32:8 NKJV

N adin Khoury was thirteen years old, five foot two, and weighed, soaking wet, probably a hundred pounds.

His attackers were teenagers, larger than Nadin, and outnumbered him seven to one.

For thirty minutes they hit, kicked, and beat him.

He never stood a chance.

Khoury's mom had recently moved the family to Philadelphia from

Minnesota. She had lost her job as a hotel maid and was looking for work. In 2000 she'd escaped war-torn Liberia. Nadin Khoury, then, was the new kid in a rough neighborhood with a mom who was an unemployed immigrant—everything a wolf pack of bullies needed to justify an attack.

The hazing began weeks earlier. They picked on him. They called his mother names. They routinely pushed, shoved, and ambushed him. Then came the all-out assault on a January day. They dragged him through the snow, stuffed him into a tree, and suspended him on a seven-foot wrought-iron fence.

Khoury survived the attack and would have likely faced a few more except for the folly of one of the bullies. He filmed the pile-on and posted it on YouTube. A passerby saw the violence and chased away the bullies. Police saw it and got involved. The troublemakers landed in jail, and the story reached the papers.

A staffer at the nationwide morning show *The View* read the account and invited Khoury to appear on the broadcast. He did. As the video of the assault played on the screen behind him, he tried to appear brave, but his lower lip quivered. "Next time maybe it could be somebody smaller than me," he said.

Unbeknown to him the producer had invited some other Philadelphians to appear on the show as well. As the YouTube video ended, the curtain opened, and three huge men walked out, members of the Philadelphia Eagles football team.

Khoury, a rabid fan, turned and smiled. One was All-Pro receiver DeSean Jackson. Jackson took a seat on the couch as close to the boy as possible and promised him, "Anytime you need us, I got two linemen right here." Khoury's eyes widened saucer-like as Jackson signed a football jersey and handed it to him. Then, in full view of every bully in America, he gave the boy his cell phone number.[1]

From that day forward Khoury has been only a call away from his personal bodyguards. Thugs think twice before they harass the kid who has an NFL football player's number on speed dial.

Pretty good offer. Who wouldn't want that type of protection?

God gives you the same promise. In fact, the writer of Hebrews quoted the words in his epistle: "For [God] has said, 'I will never leave you or forsake you.' So we can say with confidence, 'The Lord is my helper; I will not be afraid. What can anyone do to me?'" (Heb. 13:5–6 NRSV).

That last question is a troubling one. *What can anyone do to me?* You know the answers. "Lie to me." "Deceive me." "Injure me." "Terrorize me." "Bully me."

But the Scripture asks a different question. If the Lord is your helper, what can anyone do to you?

The Greek word for *helper* in this passage is *boēthos*, from *boē*, which means "a shout," and *theō*, which means "to run."[2] When you need help, God runs with a shout, "I'm coming!" He never leaves you. Ever! He never takes a break, takes a nap, or takes time off for vacation. He never leaves your side.

The job market is flat? True. But God is your helper. Your blood cell count is down? Difficult for sure, but the One who made you is with you. Is the world in fear of pandemics? Indeed it is. Still, the Almighty will never leave you or forsake you.

Consequently, everything changes! Since God is strong, you will be strong. Since he is able, you will be able. Since he has no limits, you have no limits. With the apostle you can boldly say, "The LORD is my helper; I will not fear. What can man do to me?" (v. 6 NKJV).

But there is more. The biggest—and best—news is this: God not only stays with you . . . he fights for you.

Not only does God desire that you have a chance to begin again, but he fights for you so you can and then remains your guardian throughout your journey.

Fears, diseases, pain, disappointments, and hurts come at you like a legion of hoodlums. Yet rather than run away, you turn and face them. You unsheathe the promise of God's Word and defy the enemies of God's cause. You are a grizzly and they are rats. "Get out of here, shame! Begone, guilt! Fear of death, regrets of the past, take your puny attacks elsewhere."

This is what happens when you are living the new-beginning life. You were not made to quake in fear. You were not made to be beholden to your past. You were not made to limp through life as a wimp. You are a living, breathing expression of God. What's more, he fights for you.

Is this a new thought? You've heard about the God who made you, watches you, directs you, knows you . . . but the God who fights for you? Who blazes the trail ahead of you? Who defends you? Who collapses walls, stills the sun, and rains hail on the devil and all his forces?

Did you know that God is fighting for you? That "with us is the Lord our God, to help us and to fight our battles" (2 Chron. 32:8 NKJV)? That "our God will fight for us" (Neh. 4:20 NKJV)? That the Lord will "fight against those who fight against [you]" (Ps. 35:1 NKJV)?

God fights for you. Let those four words sink in for a moment.

God. The CEO, President, King, Supreme Ruler, Absolute Monarch, Czar, Emperor, and Raja of all history. He runs interference and provides cover. He is impeccably perfect, tirelessly strong, unquestionably capable. He is endlessly joyful, wise, and willing. And he . . .

Fights. He deploys angels and commands weather. He stands down Goliaths and vacates cemeteries. He fights . . .

For. For your health, family, faith, and restoration. Are the odds against you? Is the coach against you? Is the government against you? Difficult for sure. But God fights for . . .

You. Yes, you! You with the sordid past. You with the receding hair-line. You with the absentee dad. You with the bad back, credit, or job. He fights not just for the rich, pretty, or religious. He fights for the yous of the world. Are you a *you*?

The big news of the Bible is not that you fight for God but that God fights for you. And to know this—to know that your Father fights for you—is an unparalleled source of empowerment.

When God became flesh, he fought for your soul. When Jesus faced the devil in the wilderness, he fought for your peace. When he stood up for the neglected, was he not standing up for you? When he died on the cross for your sins, he fought for your salvation. When he left the Holy Spirit to guide, strengthen, and comfort you, he was fighting for your life.

Miss this truth and you might as well plant a mailbox in the wilderness. You will be there a long time. But believe this, and watch the clouds begin to clear.

Believe this:

> [God] won't let you stumble,
> > your Guardian God won't fall asleep.
> Not on your life! Israel's
> > Guardian will never doze or sleep.
>
> God's your Guardian,
> > right at your side to protect you—
> Shielding you from sunstroke,
> > sheltering you from moonstroke.
>
> God guards you from every evil,
> > he guards your very life.
> He guards you when you leave and when you return,
> > he guards you now, he guards you always.
>
> (Ps. 121:3–8 THE MESSAGE)

This is what God wants to be for you; it is his goal for you. This is your inheritance: more victory than defeat, more joy than sadness, more hope than despair, more new-beginning days.

chapter thirteen

Keep Believing
God's Promise

But he who endures to the end shall be saved.
—MATTHEW 24:13 NKJV

L ate-night news is a poor sedative.

Last night it was for me. All I wanted was the allergen count and the basketball scores. But to get them, I had to endure the usual monologue of global misery. And last night the world seemed worse than usual.

Watching the news doesn't usually disturb me so. I'm not a gloom-and-doom sort of fellow. I feel I'm as good as the next guy in taking human tragedy with a spoon of faith. But last night . . . these days . . . the world seems dark.

Downtown streets darkened with anger and hate. Innocents trafficked, innocence lost. Homeless, jobless. Pandemic and dread. A society worn out, worked up, and wondering what comes next.

I wonder what the world will hold for my grandchildren. Their greatest concerns today are finding lightning bugs on a summer night or learning to share with their siblings. Would that their world would always be so innocent. It won't. Forests shadow every trail, and cliffs edge every turn. Every life has its share of fear. My grandchildren are no exception.

Nor are your children and grandchildren. And as appealing as a desert island or a monastery might be, seclusion is simply not the answer for facing a scary tomorrow.

Then what is? Does someone have a hand on the throttle of this train, or has the engineer bailed out just as we come in sight of dead-man's curve?

I may have found part of the answer in, of all places, the first chapter of the New Testament. I've often thought it strange that Matthew would begin his book with a genealogy. Certainly not good journalism. A list of who-sired-whom wouldn't get past most editors.

But then again, Matthew wasn't a journalist, and the Holy Spirit wasn't trying to get our attention. He was making a point. God had promised he would give a Messiah through the bloodline of Abraham (Gen. 12:3), and he did.

"Having doubts about the future?" Matthew asks. "Just take a look at the past." And with that he opens the cedar chest of Jesus' lineage and begins pulling out the dirty laundry.

Believe me, you and I would have kept some of these stories in the closet. Jesus' lineage is anything but a roll call at the Institute for Halos and Harps. Reads more like the Sunday morning occupancy at the county jail.

It begins with Abraham, the father of the nation, who more than once lied like Pinocchio just to save his neck (Gen. 12:10–20).

Abraham's grandson Jacob was slicker than a Las Vegas card shark.

He cheated his brother, lied to his father, got swindled, and then swindled his uncle (Gen. 27, 30).

Jacob's son Judah was so blinded by testosterone that he engaged the services of a streetwalker, not knowing she was his daughter-in-law! When he learned her identity, he threatened to have her burned to death for solicitation (Gen. 38).

Special mention is made of Solomon's mother, Bathsheba (who bathed in questionable places), and Solomon's father, David, who watched the bath of Bathsheba (2 Sam. 11:2–3).

Rahab was a harlot (Josh. 2:1). Ruth was a foreigner (Ruth 1.4).

Manasseh made the list, even though he forced his son to walk through fire (2 Kings 21:6). His son Amon is on the list, even though he rejected God (2 Kings 21:22).

Seems that almost half the kings were crooks, half were embezzlers, and all but a handful worshiped an idol or two for good measure.

And so reads the list of Jesus' not-so-great grandparents. Seems like the only common bond between this lot was a promise. A promise from heaven that God would use them to send his Son.

Why did God use these people? Didn't have to. Could have just laid the Savior on a doorstep. Would have been simpler that way. And why does God tell us their stories? Why does God give us an entire testament of the blunders and stumbles of his people?

Simple. He knew what you and I watched on the news last night. He knew you would fret. He knew I would worry. And he wants us to know that when the world goes wild, he stays calm.

Want proof? Read the last name on the list. In spite of all the crooked halos and tasteless gambols of his people, the last name on the list is the first one promised—Jesus.

"Joseph was the husband of Mary, and Mary was the mother of Jesus. Jesus is called the Christ" (Matt. 1:16 NCV).

Period. No more names are listed. No more are needed. As if God is announcing to a doubting world, "See, I did it. Just as I said I would. The plan succeeded."

The famine couldn't starve it.

Four hundred years of Egyptian slavery couldn't oppress it.

Wilderness wanderings couldn't lose it.

Babylonian captivity couldn't stop it.

Clay-footed pilgrims couldn't spoil it.

The promise of the Messiah threads its way through forty-two generations of rough-cut stones, forming a necklace fit for the King who came. Just as promised.

And the promise remains.

"Those people who keep their faith until the end will be saved" (Matt. 24:13 NCV), Joseph's child assures.

"In this world you will have trouble, but be brave! I have defeated the world" (John 16:33 NCV).

The engineer has not abandoned the train. Nuclear war is no threat to God. Yo-yo economies don't intimidate the heavens. Immoral leaders have never derailed the plan.

God keeps his promise.

See for yourself. In the manger. He's there.

See for yourself. In the tomb. He's gone.

part four

Influence
Your World

You were made to make a difference. Do you desire to do so?

Start with your head. Scripture places a premium on what you know. "We have come to know and believe the love God has for us" (1 John 4:16 NLV).

Jesus did not say, "You shall feel the truth," "You shall experience the truth," or "You shall emotionally bond with the truth." Rather he promised, "You will *know* the truth, and the truth will make you free" (John 8:32 NCV, emphasis mine).

Use your head, but don't stop there. What starts in the head continues in the heart.

Facts evolve into faith. Isn't this what happened to Timothy? Paul commended him: "You, however, continue in the things you have learned and become convinced of, knowing from whom you have learned them" (2 Tim. 3:14 NASB).

See the knowing-believing sequence again? ". . . in the things you have learned and become convinced of . . ."

What begins in the head must descend into the heart. Doesn't it always? Can't we simply assume that the right knowledge will lead to the right life? It didn't for Felix. During the life of the apostle Paul, Felix served as governor. When Paul was imprisoned, Felix had the authority to release him. But Paul fascinated Felix. What's more, Felix was tutored by Paul. "[Felix] used to send for him quite often and converse with him" (Acts 24:26 NASB).

Can you imagine studying Scripture with Paul? This is Pelé showing you how to kick a soccer ball. Monet giving you art lessons. Ernest Hemingway reading your theme paper. Felix benefited. He gained a "more exact knowledge about the Way" (Acts 24:22 NASB). He knew the facts. He heard the truth. He filled his mind with knowledge.

But Felix refused to let the facts touch his heart. "Felix became frightened and said, 'Go away for the present, and when I find time I will summon you'" (Acts 24:25 NASB).

The governor enjoyed the intellectual chitchat, academic stimulus, philosophical sparring. Facts for the head? Okay. But a change of the heart? No way. Felix erected a barricade at his Adam's apple. Paul may have been thinking of him when he spoke of people who are "always learning but never able to come to a knowledge of the truth" (2 Tim. 3:7).

Some years ago a Christian scholar and an Israeli guide cohosted a Bible lands tour. The guide knew details about the life of Jesus the way Beethoven knew piano keys. He grew up in the shadow of the Mount of Olives and made a living reciting facts about Jesus. But the guide didn't believe in him. Toward the end of the trip, the scholar gave him this counsel: "You know more about Jesus than anyone I know. You just need to let the facts sink one foot lower."

May I show you how this works? Suppose you acquire new knowledge about God's grace. You quarry a jewel from 1 John: "The blood of Jesus, his Son, cleanses us from all sin" (1:7 NLT). Christ does for your sins what windshield wipers do for raindrops—he continually removes them.

Wow. What a phenomenal fact to know. But what will you do with it? Jot it down in the margin of your Bible? Mention it in conversations? Underline the scripture? Good starts. But so far all you've done is work with your head.

Press the elevator button, and let the truth descend into your heart. Go from academic to personal. "Oh, Lord, thank you. Every sin perpetually cleansed. Today's greed, yesterday's gripes—all clean. By your mercy I am as pure as the angels of heaven. What a gift."

That's called receiving. Refuse to be a Felix, full of facts. And choose to be a disciple, flowing with faith.

As you receive, wonders occur. Smiles replace frowns. Joy eclipses anxiety. Rest replaces panic. And, in time, facts in your head will become faith in your heart and create the fruit of your hands.

Yes, "doing" matters to God. But "doing" follows receiving. Paul carefully presents the proper order:

"The things which you *learned* and *received* and heard and saw in me, these *do*, and the God of peace will be with you (Phil. 4:9 NKJV, emphasis mine).

Learn.

Receive.

Do.

Facts enter your head, descend into your heart as faith, and exit your hands as energy. Deeds of kindness. Acts of generosity. Calling on the sick. Volunteering for the committee. Baking pies for Max. (Just kidding.) The work of the hands follows the filling of the head and heart.

You were made to make a difference. Let Christ make a difference in you, and you will do the same in the world.

chapter fourteen

Be You

Each person is given something to
do that shows who God is.
—1 CORINTHIANS 12:7 THE MESSAGE

N
o one else has your "you-ness." No one else in all history has
your unique history. No one else in God's great design has your
divine design. No one else shares your blend of personality,
ability, and ancestry. When God made you, the angels stood in awe and
declared, "We've never seen one like that before." And they never will
again. Your journey is one of a kind.

You are heaven's first and final attempt at you. You are matchless,
unprecedented, and unequaled.

Consequently, on your new-beginning journey you can do something
no one else can do in a fashion no one else can.

Others can manage a team but not with your style. Others can cook a meal but not with your flair. Others can teach kids, tell stories, aviate airplanes. You aren't the only person with your skill. But you are the only one with your version of your skill. You entered the world uniquely equipped. You were "knit . . . together . . . woven together in the dark of the womb" (Ps. 139:13, 15 NLT), "intricately *and* skillfully formed [as if embroidered with many colors]" (v. 15 AMP).

Each of us—not some of us, a few of us, or the elite among us. Each of us has a *special way*—a facility, a natural strength, a tendency, or an inclination. A beauty that longs to be revealed and released. An oak within the acorn, pressing against the walls of its shell. This "special way" is quick to feel the wind at its back. It is the work for which you are ideally suited.

This is your destiny. This is you at your best. When you stand at the intersection of your skill and God's call, you are standing at the corner of Begin Again Avenue and Second Chance Boulevard, where Noah stood after the flood.

Many people stop short of their destiny. They settle for someone else's story. "Grandpa was a butcher, Dad was a butcher, so I guess I'll be a butcher." "Everyone I know is in farming, so I guess I'm supposed to farm." Consequently, they risk leading dull, joyless, and fruitless lives. They never sing the song God wrote for their voices. They never cross a finish line with heavenward-stretched arms and declare, "I was made to do this!"

They fit in, settle in, and blend in. But they never find their call. Don't make the same mistake.

"It is God himself who has made us what we are and given us new lives from Christ Jesus; and long ages ago he planned that we should spend these lives in helping others" (Eph. 2:10 TLB). Your existence is not accidental. Your skills are not incidental. God "shaped each person in turn" (Ps. 33:15 THE MESSAGE).

Everybody gets a gift. And these gifts come in different doses and combinations. "Each person is given something to do that shows who God is" (1 Cor. 12:7 THE MESSAGE).

Our inheritance is grace based and equal. But our assignments are tailor-made. No two snowflakes are the same. No two fingerprints are the same. Why would two skill sets be the same? No wonder Paul said, "Make sure you understand what the Master wants" (Eph. 5:17 THE MESSAGE).

Do you understand what your Master wants? Do you know what makes you, you? Have you identified the features that distinguish you from every other human who has inhaled oxygen?

You have an "acreage" to develop, a lot in life. So "make a careful exploration of who you are and the work you have been given, and then sink yourself into that" (Gal. 6:4 THE MESSAGE).

You be you. No one else is like you. Imagine a classroom of kids on a given day in a given school. Ten of the twenty-five students are fighting to stay awake. Ten others are alert but ready to leave. Five students are not only awake and alert, but they don't want the class to end. They even do odd things like extra homework or tutoring. What class was that intriguing to you?

"If anyone ministers, let him do it as with *the ability* which God supplies" (1 Peter 4:11 NKJV, emphasis mine). Ability reveals destiny. What is your ability? What do you do well? What do people ask you to do again? What task comes easily? What topic keeps your attention?

Your skill set is your road map. It leads you to your territory. Take note of your strengths. They are bread crumbs that will lead you out of the wilderness. God loves you too much to give you a job and not the skills. Identify yours.

Look for ways to align your job with your skills. This may take time. This may take several conversations with your boss. This may take trial and error . . . but don't give up. Not every tuba player has the skills to direct the orchestra. If you can, then do. If you can't, blast away on your tuba with delight.

"Stir up the gift of God which is *in you*" (2 Tim. 1:6 NKJV, emphasis mine).

You be you. Don't be your parents or grandparents. You can admire them, appreciate them, and learn from them. But you cannot be them. You aren't them. "Don't compare yourself with others. Each of you must take responsibility for doing the creative best you can with your own life" (Gal. 6:4–5 THE MESSAGE).

Jesus was insistent on this. After the resurrection he appeared to some of his followers. He gave Peter a specific pastoral assignment that included great sacrifice. The apostle responded by pointing at John and saying, "'Lord, what about him?' Jesus answered, 'If I want him to live until I come back, that is not your business. You follow me'" (John 21:21–22 NCV). In other words don't occupy yourself with another person's assignment; stay focused on your own.

A little boy named Adam wanted to be like his friend Bobby. Adam loved the way Bobby walked and talked. Bobby, however, wanted to be like Charlie. Something about Charlie's stride and accent intrigued him. Charlie, on the other hand, was impressed with Danny. Charlie wanted to look and sound like Danny. Danny, of all things, had a hero as well: Adam. He wanted to be just like Adam.

So Adam was imitating Bobby, who was imitating Charlie, who was imitating Danny, who was imitating Adam.

Turns out, all Adam had to do was be himself.[1]

So when you begin again, stay in your own lane. Run your own race. Nothing good happens when you compare and compete. God does not judge you according to the talents of others. He judges you according to yours. His yardstick for measuring faithfulness is how faithful you are with your own gifts. You are not responsible for the nature of your gift. But you are responsible for how you use it.

So run! Move forward by faith! Find your lot in life and live in it.

You be you.

chapter fifteen

Share What God Has Given

Love . . . believes all things.
—1 CORINTHIANS 13:4–7 NASB

B y all rules, Skinner was a dead man." With these words Arthur
Bressi begins his retelling of the day he found his best friend
in a World War II Japanese concentration camp. The two
were high-school buddies. They grew up together in Mount Carmel,
Pennsylvania—playing ball, skipping school, double-dating. Arthur and
Skinner were inseparable. It made sense, then, that when one joined
the army, the other would as well. They rode the same troopship to the
Philippines. That's where they were separated. Skinner was on Bataan

when it fell to the Japanese in 1942. Arthur Bressi was captured a month later.

Through the prison grapevine, Arthur learned the whereabouts of his friend. Skinner was near death in a nearby camp. Arthur volunteered for work detail in the hope that his company might pass through the other camp. One day they did.

Arthur requested and was given five minutes to find and speak to his friend. He knew to go to the sick side of the camp. It was divided into two sections—one for those expected to recover, the other for those given no hope. Those expected to die lived in a barracks called "zero ward." That's where Arthur found Skinner. He called his name, and out of the barracks walked the seventy-nine-pound shadow of the friend he had once known.

As he writes:

I stood at the wire fence of the Japanese prisoner-of-war camp on Luzon and watched my childhood buddy, caked in filth and racked with the pain of multiple diseases, totter toward me. He was dead; only his boisterous spirit hadn't left his body. I wanted to look away, but couldn't. His blue eyes, watery and dulled, locked on me and wouldn't let go.[1]

Malaria. Amebic dysentery. Pellagra. Scurvy. Beriberi. Skinner's body was a dormitory for tropical diseases. He couldn't eat. He couldn't drink. He was nearly gone.

Arthur didn't know what to do or say. His five minutes were nearly up. He began to finger the heavy knot of the handkerchief tied around his neck. In it was his high-school class ring. At the risk of punishment he'd smuggled the ring into camp. Knowing the imminence of disease and the scarcity of treatment, he had been saving it to barter for medicine or food for himself. But one look at Skinner, and he knew he couldn't save it any longer.

As he told his friend good-bye, he slipped the ring through the fence into Skinner's frail hand and told him to "wheel and deal" with it. Skinner objected, but Arthur insisted. He turned and left, not knowing if he would ever see his friend alive again.

What kind of love would do something like that? It's one thing to give a gift to the healthy. It's one thing to share a treasure with the strong. But to give your best to the weak, to entrust your treasure to the dying—that's saying something. Indeed, that's saying something to them. "I believe in you," the gesture declares. "Don't despair. Don't give up. I believe in you." It's no wonder Paul included this phrase in his definition of love: "[Love] believes all things" (1 Cor. 13:7 NASB).

Do you know anyone who is standing on Skinner's side of the fence? If your child is having trouble in school, you do. If your husband struggles with depression or your wife has been laid off, you do. If you have a friend with cancer, if the class mocks your classmate, if your son didn't make the squad, if you know anyone who is afraid or has failed or is frail, then you know someone who needs a ring of belief.

And, what's more, you can give them one. You may, by virtue of your words or ways, change that person's life forever.

Arthur did. Want to know what happened to Skinner? He took the ring and buried it in the barracks floor. The next day he took the biggest risk of his life. He approached the "kindest" of the guards and passed him the ring through the fence. *"Takai?"* the guard asked. "Is it valuable?" Skinner assured him that it was. The soldier smiled and slipped the ring into a pocket and left. A couple of days later he walked past Skinner and let a packet drop at his feet. Sulfanilamide tablets. A day later he returned with limes to combat the scurvy. Then came a new pair of pants and some canned beef. Within three weeks Skinner was on his feet. Within three months he was taken to the healthy side of the sick camp. In time he was able to work. As far as Skinner knew, he was the only American ever to leave the zero ward alive.

All because of a ring. All because someone believed in him.

I know what some of you are thinking. You're looking at Arthur and Skinner and wishing your situation were so easy. Skinner was a dying man but a good man, a good friend. How do you believe in someone who isn't? How do you believe in a man who cheats on you or an employee who swindles you? Does love ignore all things? I don't think so. This passage is not a call to naiveté or blindness. It is, however, a call for us to give to others what God has given us.

Skinner is not the only person to be given a ring, you know. You have one on your finger as well. Your heavenly Father placed it there. Jesus described the moment when he told the story of the prodigal son.

The tale involves a wealthy father and a willful son. The boy prematurely takes his inheritance and moves to Las Vegas and there wastes the money on slot machines and call girls. As fast as you can say "blackjack," he is broke. Too proud to go home, he gets a job sweeping horse stables at the racetrack. When he finds himself tasting some of their oats and thinking, *Hmm, a dash of salt and this wouldn't be too bad*, he realizes enough is enough. It's time to go home. The gardener at his father's house does better than this. So off he goes, rehearsing his repentance speech every step of the way.

But the father has other ideas. "When he was still a great way off, his father saw him." The dad was looking for the boy, always craning his neck, ever hoping the boy would show, and when he did, when the father saw the familiar figure on the trail, he "had compassion, and ran and fell on his neck and kissed him."

We don't expect such a response. We expect crossed arms and a furrowed brow. At best a guarded handshake. At least a stern lecture. But the father gives none of these. Instead he gives gifts. "Bring out the best robe . . . a ring . . . sandals. . . . And bring the fatted calf . . . and let us eat and be merry" (Luke 15:11–23 NKJV). Robe, sandals, calf, and . . . Did you see it? A ring.

Before the boy has a chance to wash his hands, he has a ring to put on his finger. In Christ's day rings were more than gifts; they were symbols of delegated sovereignty. The bearer of the ring could speak on behalf of the giver. It was used to press a seal into soft wax to validate a transaction. The one who wore the ring conducted business in the name of the one who gave it.

Would you have done this? Would you have given this prodigal son power-of-attorney privileges over your affairs? Would you have entrusted him with a credit card? Would you have given him this ring?

Before you start questioning the wisdom of the father, remember, in this story you are the boy. When you came home to God, you were given authority to conduct business in your heavenly Father's name.

When you speak truth, you are God's ambassador.

As you steward the money he gives, you are his business manager.

When you declare forgiveness, you are his priest.

As you stir the healing of the body or the soul, you are his physician.

And when you pray, he listens to you as a father listens to his child. You have a voice in the household of God. He has given you his ring.

The only thing more remarkable than the giving of the ring is the fact that he hasn't taken it back! Weren't there times when he could have?

When you promoted your cause and forgot his. When you spoke lies and not truth. When you took his gifts and used them for personal gain. When you took the bus back to Las Vegas and found yourself seduced into the world of lights, luck, and long nights. Couldn't he have taken the ring? Absolutely. But did he? Do you still have a Bible? Are you still allowed to pray? Do you still have a dollar to manage or a skill to use? Then it appears he still wants you to have the ring. It appears he still believes in you!

He hasn't given up on you. He hasn't turned away. He hasn't walked out. He could have. Others would have. But he hasn't. God believes in you. And, I wonder, could you take some of the belief that he has in you and share it with someone else? Could you believe in someone?

In the prison camp Arthur gave Skinner much more than a ring; he gave him a proclamation, a judgment that said, "You are worth this much to me! Your life is worth saving. Your life is worth living." He believed in him and, as a result, gave Skinner the means and the courage to save himself.

You and I have the privilege to do for others what Arthur did for Skinner and what God does for us. How do we show people that we believe in them?

Show up. Nothing takes the place of your presence. Letters are nice. Phone calls are special, but being there in the flesh sends a message.

Do you believe in your kids? Then show up. Show up at their games. Show up at their plays. Show up at their recitals. It may not be possible to make each one, but it's sure worth the effort. An elder in our church supports me with his presence. Whenever I speak at an area congregation, he'll show up. Does nothing. Says little. Just takes a seat in a pew and smiles when we make eye contact. It means a lot to me.

Listen up. You don't have to speak to encourage. The Bible says, "It is best to listen much, speak little" (James 1:19 TLB). We tend to speak much and listen little. There is a time to speak. But there is also a time to be quiet. That's what my father did. Dropping a fly ball may not be a big deal to most people, but if you are thirteen years old and have aspirations of the big leagues, it is a big deal. Not only was it my second error of the game, but it also allowed the winning run to score.

I didn't even go back to the dugout. I turned around in the middle of left field and climbed over the fence. I was halfway home when my dad found me. He didn't say a word. Just pulled over to the side of the road, leaned across the seat, and opened the passenger door. We didn't speak. We didn't need to. We both knew the world had come to an end. When we got home, I went straight to my room, and he went straight to the kitchen. Presently he appeared in front of me with cookies and milk. He took a seat on the bed, and we broke bread together. Somewhere in the dunking of the cookies, I began to realize that life and my father's love would go on. In the economy of male adolescence, if you love the guy who drops the ball, then you really love him. My skill as a baseball player didn't improve, but my confidence in Dad's love did. Dad never said a word. But he did show up. He did listen up. To bring out the best in others, do the same, and then, when appropriate:

Speak up. Nathaniel Hawthorne came home heartbroken. He'd just been fired from his job in the custom house. His wife, rather than responding with anxiety, surprised him with joy. "Now you can write your book!"

He wasn't so positive. "And what shall we live on while I'm writing it?"

To his amazement she opened a drawer and revealed a wad of money she'd saved out of her housekeeping budget. "I always knew you were a man of genius," she told him. "I always knew you'd write a masterpiece."

She believed in her husband. And because she did, he wrote. And because he wrote, every library in America has a copy of *The Scarlet Letter* by Nathaniel Hawthorne.[2]

You have the power to change someone's life simply by the words you speak. "Death and life are in the power of the tongue" (Prov. 18:21 NKJV). That's why Paul urges you and me to be careful. "When you talk, do not say harmful things, but say what people need—words that will help others become stronger" (Eph. 4:29 NCV).

Before you speak, ask: Will what I'm about to say help others become stronger? You have the ability, with your words, to make a person stronger. Your words are to their soul what a vitamin is to their body. If you had food and saw someone starving, would you not share it? If you had water and saw someone dying of thirst, would you not give it? Of course you would. Then won't you do the same for their hearts? Your words are food and water! Do not withhold encouragement from the discouraged. Do not keep affirmation from the beaten down! Speak words that make people stronger. Believe in them as God has believed in you.

You may save someone's life.

Arthur did. His friend Skinner survived. Both men returned home to Mount Carmel. One day soon after their arrival, Skinner came over for a visit. He had a gift with him. A small box. Arthur knew immediately what it was. It was an exact copy of the high-school ring. After a lame attempt at humor—"Don't lose that; it cost me eighteen dollars"—he gave his friend a warm smile and said, "That ring, Artie . . . it saved my life."[3]

May someone say the same to you.

May you say the same to God.

chapter sixteen

Love Those
in Need

*Whenever you did one of these things to someone
overlooked or ignored, that was me—you did it to me.*
—MATTHEW 25:40 THE MESSAGE

A t 7:51 a.m., January 12, 2007, a young musician took his position
against a wall in a Washington, DC, metro station. He wore
jeans, a long-sleeved T-shirt, and a Washington Nationals baseball cap. He opened a violin case, removed his instrument, threw a few
dollars and pocket change into the case as seed money, and began to play.

He played for the next forty-three minutes. He performed six clas-
sical pieces. During that time more than a thousand people passed by.

They tossed in money to the total of $32.17. Of the thousand people seven—only seven—paused longer than sixty seconds. And of the seven, one—only one—recognized the violinist Joshua Bell.

Three days prior to this metro appearance staged by the *Washington Post*, Bell filled Boston's Symphony Hall, where just fairly good tickets went for $100 a seat. Two weeks after the experiment he played for a standing-room-only audience in Bethesda, Maryland. Joshua Bell's talents can command $1,000 a minute. That day in the subway station, he barely earned enough to buy a cheap pair of shoes.

You can't fault the instrument. He played a Stradivarius built in the golden period of Stradivari's career. It's worth $3.5 million. You can't fault the music. Bell successfully played a piece from Johann Sebastian Bach that Bell called "one of the greatest achievements of any man in history."

But scarcely anyone noticed. No one expected majesty in such a context. Shoeshine stand to one side, kiosk to the other. People buying magazines, newspapers, chocolate bars, and lotto tickets. And who had time? This was a workday. This was the Washington workforce. Government workers mainly, on their way to budget meetings and management sessions. Who had time to notice beauty in the midst of busyness? Most did not.[1]

Most of us will someday realize that we didn't either. From the perspective of heaven we'll look back on these days—these busy, cluttered days—and realize, *That was Jesus playing the violin. That was Jesus wearing the ragged clothes. That was Jesus in the orphanage . . . in the jail . . . in the cardboard shanty. The person needing my help was Jesus.*

There are many reasons to help people in need.

"Benevolence is good for the world."

"We all float on the same ocean. When the tide rises, it benefits everyone."

"To deliver someone from poverty is to unleash that person's potential as a researcher, educator, or doctor."

"As we reduce poverty and disease, we reduce war and atrocities. Healthy, happy people don't hurt each other."

Compassion has a dozen advocates.

But for the Christian none is higher than this: when we love those in need, we are loving Jesus. It is a mystery beyond science, a truth beyond statistics. But it is a message that Jesus made crystal clear: when we love them, we love him.

This is the theme of his final sermon. The message he saved until last. He must want this point imprinted on our consciences. He depicted the final judgment scene. The last day, the great Day of Judgment. On that day Jesus will issue an irresistible command. All will come. From sunken ships and forgotten cemeteries, they will come. From royal tombs and grassy battlefields, they will come. From Abel, the first to die, to the person being buried at the moment Jesus calls, every human in history will be present.

All the angels will be present. The whole heavenly universe will witness the event. A staggering denouement. Jesus at some point will "separate them one from another, as a shepherd divides his sheep from the goats" (Matt. 25:32 NKJV). Shepherds do this. They walk among the flock and, one by one, with the use of a staff direct goats in one direction and sheep in the other.

Graphic, this thought of the Good Shepherd stepping through the flock of humanity. You. Me. Our parents and kids. "Max, go this way." "Ronaldo, over there." "Maria, this side."

How can one envision this moment without the sudden appearance of this urgent question: What determines his choice? How does Jesus separate the people?

Jesus gives the answer. Those on the right, the sheep, will be those who fed him when he was hungry, brought him water when he was thirsty, gave him lodging when he was lonely, clothing when he was naked, and comfort when he was sick or imprisoned. The sign of the saved is their concern for those in need. Compassion does not save them—or us. Salvation is the work of Christ. Compassion is the consequence of salvation.

The sheep will react with a sincere question: When? When did we feed, visit, clothe, or comfort you? (vv. 34–39).

Jesus' answer will sound something like this: "Remember when you got off the subway? It was a wintry Washington morning. Commuters were bundled and busy and focused on their work. You were, too, mind you. But then you saw me. Yes, that was me! Standing between the coffee kiosk and the newsstand—that was me. I was wearing a baseball cap and a scarf and playing a fiddle. The mob rushed past as if I were a plastic plant. But you stopped. I knew you were busy. You looked at your watch twice. But still you stopped and remembered me. You stepped over to the coffee stand, bought me a cup, and brought it over. I want you to know I never forgot that."

Jesus will recount, one by one, all the acts of kindness. Every deed done to improve the lot of another person. Even the small ones. In fact, they all seem small. Giving water. Offering food. Sharing clothing. As Chrysostom pointed out, "We do not hear, 'I was sick and you *healed* me,' or 'I was in prison and you *liberated* me.'"[2] The works of mercy are simple deeds. And yet in these simple deeds, we serve Jesus. Astounding, this truth: we serve Christ by serving needy people.

The Jerusalem church understood this. How else can we explain their explosion across the world? We've only considered a handful of their stories. What began on Pentecost with the 120 disciples spilled into every corner of the world. Antioch. Corinth. Ephesus. Rome. The book of Acts, unlike other New Testament books, has no conclusion. That's because the work has not been finished.

Many years ago I heard a woman discuss this work. She visited a Catholic church in downtown Miami, Florida, in 1979. The small sanctuary overflowed with people. I was surprised. The event wasn't publicized. I happened to hear of the noon-hour presentation through a friend. I was living only a few blocks from the church. I showed up a few minutes early in hopes of a front-row seat. I should have arrived two hours early. People packed every pew and aisle. Some sat in windowsills. I found a spot against the back wall and waited. I don't know if the air-conditioning was broken or nonexistent, but the windows were open, and the south coast air was stuffy. The audience was chatty and restless. Yet when she entered the room, all stirring stopped.

No music. No long introduction. No fanfare from any public officials. No entourage. Just three, maybe four, younger versions of herself, the local priest, and her.

The father issued a brief word of welcome and told a joke about placing a milk crate behind the lectern so we could see his guest. He wasn't kidding. He positioned it, and she stepped up, and those blue eyes looked out at us. What a face. Vertical lines chiseled around her mouth. Her nose, larger than most women would prefer. Thin lips, as if drawn with a pencil, and a smile naked of pretense.

She wore her characteristic white Indian sari with a blue border that represented the Missionaries of Charity, the order she had founded in 1950. Her sixty-nine years had bent her already small frame. But there was nothing small about Mother Teresa's presence.

"Give me your unborn children," she offered. (Opening words or just the ones I remember most? I don't know.) "Don't abort them. If you cannot raise them, I will. They are precious to God."

Who would have ever pegged this slight Albanian woman as a change agent? Born in a cauldron of ethnic strife, the Balkans. Shy and introverted as a child. Of fragile health. One of three children. Daughter of a generous but unremarkable businessman. Yet somewhere along her journey, she became convinced that Jesus walked in the "distressing disguise of the poor," and she set out to love him by loving them. In 1989 she told a reporter that her Missionaries had picked up around fifty-four thousand people from the streets of Calcutta and that twenty-three thousand or so had died in their care.[3]

I wonder if God creates people like Mother Teresa so he can prove his point: "See, you can do something on your life's journey that will outlive you."

There are several billion reasons to consider his challenge. Some of them live in your neighborhood; others live in jungles you can't find and have names you can't pronounce. Some of them play in cardboard slums or sell sex on a busy street. Some of them walk three hours for water or wait all day for a shot of penicillin. Some of them brought their woes on themselves, and others inherited the mess from their parents.

None of us can help everyone. But all of us can help someone. And when we help them, we serve Jesus.

Who would want to miss a chance to do that?

> Then the King will say to those on his right, "Come, you who are blessed by my Father, inherit the Kingdom prepared for you from the creation of the world. For I was hungry, and you fed me. I was thirsty, and you gave me a drink. I was a stranger, and you invited me into your home. I was naked, and you gave me clothing. I was sick, and you cared for me. I was in prison, and you visited me." (Matt. 25:34–36 NLT)

O Lord, where did I see you yesterday . . . and didn't recognize you? Where will I encounter you today . . . and fail to identify you? O my Father, give me eyes to see, a heart to respond, and hands and feet to serve you wherever you encounter me! Transform me, Lord, by your Spirit into a servant of Christ, who delights to meet the needs of those around me. Make me a billboard of your grace, a living advertisement for the riches of your compassion. I long to hear you say to me one day, "Well done, good and faithful servant." And I pray that *today* I would be that faithful servant who does well at doing good. In Jesus' name I pray, amen.

chapter seventeen

Make a Difference

I have fought the good fight, I have
finished the race, I have kept the faith.
—2 TIMOTHY 4:7

Unfavorable winds blow the ship off course, and when they do, the sailors spot uncharted islands. They see half a dozen mounds rising out of the blue South Seas waters. The captain orders the men to drop anchor and goes ashore. He is a robust man with a barrel chest, full beard, and curious soul.

On the first island he sees nothing but sadness. Underfed children. Tribes in conflict. No farming or food development, no treatment for the sick, and no schools. Just simple, needy people.

The second and following islands reveal more of the same. The captain sighs at what he sees. "This is no life for these people." But what can he do?

Then he steps onto the last and largest island. The people are healthy and well fed. Irrigation systems nourish their fields, and roads connect the villages. The children have bright eyes and strong bodies. The captain asks the chief for an explanation. How has this island moved so far ahead of the others?

The chief, who is smaller than the captain but every bit his equal in confidence, gives a quick response: "Father Benjamin. He educated us in everything from agriculture to health. He built schools and clinics and dug wells."

The captain asks, "Can you take me to see him?"

The chief nods and signals for two tribesmen to join him. They guide the captain over a jungle ridge to a simple, expansive medical clinic. It is equipped with clean beds and staffed with trained caretakers. They show the captain the shelves of medicine and introduce him to the staff. The captain, though impressed, sees nothing of Father Benjamin. He repeats his request. "I would like to see Father Benjamin. Can you take me to where he lives?"

The three natives look puzzled. They confer among themselves. After several minutes the chief invites, "Follow us to the other side of the island." They walk along the shoreline until they reach a series of fishponds. Canals connect the ponds to the ocean. As the tide rises, fish pass from the ocean into the ponds. The islanders then lower canal gates and trap the fish for harvest.

Again the captain is amazed. He meets fishermen and workers, gate-keepers and net casters. But he sees nothing of Father Benjamin. He wonders if he is making himself clear.

"I don't see Father Benjamin. Please take me to where he lives."

The trio talks privately again. After some discussion the chief offers,

"Let's go up the mountain." They lead the captain up a steep, narrow path. After many twists and turns the path deposits them in front of a grass-roofed chapel. The voice of the chief is soft and earnest. "He has taught us about God."

He escorts the captain inside and shows him the altar, a large wooden cross, several rows of benches, and a Bible.

"Is this where Father Benjamin lives?" the captain asks.

The men nod and smile.

"May I talk to him?"

Their faces grow suddenly serious. "Oh, that would be impossible."

"Why?"

"He died many years ago."

The bewildered captain stares at the men. "I asked to see him, and you showed me a clinic, some fish farms, and this chapel. You said nothing of his death."

"You didn't ask about his death," the chief explains. "You asked to see where he lives. We showed you."

part five

Nurture an Eternal Perspective

I spent a year in a subway one hour. I and a dozen or so other passengers boarded a train in a suburb of São Paulo, Brazil. Midnight was near, train station quiet, and our expectations simple: to get home safely.

We did, eventually. But only after the train, for reasons I never discovered, came to a lurching stop in a tunnel. The lights blacked out. The motors shut down. And a car of strangers sat in the inky night of an underground passage.

You can anticipate our thoughts. A few groans. Someone next to a girlfriend made a joke. Another commuter expressed frustration: "This happens every time I take this train."

We all expected the engines to reboot and lights to reignite quickly. When they didn't, our concerns heightened. At least mine did. Trapped underground in a confined space with a group of strangers. I checked my wallet, held my breath, and made a mental note to take the bus next time.

No one wants to be stuck in the dark, trapped in a tunnel with no word from the outside. But millions of people feel and fear that they are.

Their world seems like a stalled subway train: going nowhere with no message from the conductor. This is the picture of a life with no heaven.

A heaven-less life enjoys no light at the end of the tunnel, no hope of disembarking at the end of the ride, no home at the end of the journey. A life with no heaven chisels an epitaph like this one found on a headstone in a British cemetery: "I was nothing. I am nothing. So thou who art shall still be alive, eat, drink, and be merry."

A life without heaven feels stuck. A society with no heaven results in chaos. Jesus once told a parable of two servants. The first one thought the master was coming home; the second didn't. The servant who expected the master kept the house in order. The one who didn't began "to beat his fellow servants, and to eat and drink with the drunkards" (Matt. 24:49 NKJV). No-coming master often results in no-good behavior. We hurt ourselves and others.

That's why end-time teaching dominates the Bible. Jesus didn't occasionally or casually refer to heaven. In fact, two-thirds of his parables relate to resurrection and the afterlife. He wants us to know this train is moving toward the final station. Everything changes when we know we are headed somewhere. Everything changed when we discovered the subway train was.

"Remain in your seats," the voice crackled over the radio. "We will be moving soon." And we did and we were. Lights blinked, engines cranked, and we lunged forward as suddenly as we had stopped. We sighed, smiled at one another, and gave thanks for the forward motion.

Happy are the homeward bound.

chapter eighteen

Reserve Judgment
of Life's Storms

Now I know in part; then I shall know
fully, even as I am fully known.
—1 CORINTHIANS 13:12

Would you buy a house if you were allowed to see only one of its rooms? Would you purchase a car if you were permitted to see only its tires and a taillight? Would you pass judgment on a book after reading only one paragraph?

Nor would I.

Good judgment requires a broad picture. Not only is that true in purchasing houses, cars, and books; it's true in evaluating life. One failure doesn't make a person a failure; one achievement doesn't make a person a success.

"The end of a matter is better than its beginning,"[1] penned the sage.

"Be . . . patient in affliction,"[2] echoed the apostle Paul.

"Don't judge a phrase by one word," stated the woodcutter.

The woodcutter? Oh, you may not know him. Let me present him to you.

I met him in Brazil. He was introduced to me by a friend who knew that I needed patience. Denalyn and I were six months into a five-year stint in Brazil, and I was frustrated. My fascination with Rio de Janeiro had turned into exasperation with words I couldn't speak and a culture I didn't understand.

"*Tenha paciência*," Maria would tell me. "Just be patient." She was my Portuguese instructor. But more than that she was a calm voice in a noisy storm. With maternal persistence she corrected my pronunciation and helped me learn to love her homeland.

Once in the midst of a frustrating week of trying to get our goods out of customs (which eventually took three months), she gave me this story as a homework assignment. It helped my attitude far more than it helped my Portuguese.

It's a simple fable. Yet for those of us who try to pass judgment on life with only one day's evidence, the message is profound. I've done nothing to embellish it; I've only translated it. I pray that it will remind you, as it did me, that patience is the greater courage.

Once there was an old man who lived in a tiny village. Although poor, he was envied by all, for he owned a beautiful white horse. Even the king coveted his treasure. A horse like this had never been seen before—such was its splendor, its majesty, its strength.

People offered fabulous prices for the steed, but the old man always refused. "This horse is not a horse to me," he would tell them. "It is a person. How could you sell a person? He is a friend, not a possession. How could you sell a friend?" The man was poor, and the temptation was great. But he never sold the horse.

One morning he found that the horse was not in the stable. All the village came to see him. "You old fool," they scoffed, "we told you that someone would steal your horse. We warned you that you would be robbed. You are so poor. How could you ever hope to protect such a valuable animal? It would have been better to have sold him. You could have gotten whatever price you wanted. No amount would have been too high. Now the horse is gone, and you've been cursed with misfortune."

The old man responded, "Don't speak too quickly. Say only that the horse is not in the stable. That is all we know; the rest is judgment. If I've been cursed or not, how can you know? How can you judge?"

The people contested, "Don't make us out to be fools! We may not be philosophers, but great philosophy is not needed. The simple fact that your horse is gone is a curse."

The old man spoke again. "All I know is that the stable is empty, and the horse is gone. The rest I don't know. Whether it be a curse or a blessing, I can't say. All we can see is a fragment. Who can say what will come next?"

The people of the village laughed. They thought that the man was crazy. They had always thought he was a fool; if he wasn't, he would have sold the horse and lived off the money. But instead he was a poor wood-cutter, an old man still cutting firewood and dragging it out of the forest and selling it. He lived hand to mouth in the misery of poverty. Now he had proven that he was, indeed, a fool.

After fifteen days the horse returned. He hadn't been stolen; he had run away into the forest. Not only had he returned; he had brought a dozen wild horses with him. Once again the village people gathered around the woodcutter and spoke. "Old man, you were right and we were wrong. What we thought was a curse was a blessing. Please forgive us."

The man responded, "Once again you go too far. Say only that the horse is back. State only that a dozen horses returned with him, but don't judge. How do you know if this is a blessing or not? You see only a fragment. Unless you know the whole story, how can you judge? You read only one page of a book. Can you judge the whole book? You read only one word of a phrase. Can you understand the entire phrase?

"Life is so vast, yet you judge all of life with one page or one word. All you have is a fragment! Don't say that this is a blessing. No one knows. I am content with what I know. I am not perturbed by what I don't."

"Maybe the old man is right," they said to one another. So they said little. But down deep they knew he was wrong. They knew it was a blessing. Twelve wild horses had returned with one horse. With a little bit of work, the animals could be broken and trained and sold for much money.

The old man had a son, an only son. The young man began to break the wild horses. After a few days he fell from one of the horses and broke both legs. Once again the villagers gathered around the old man and cast their judgments.

"You were right," they said. "You proved you were right. The dozen horses were not a blessing. They were a curse. Your only son has broken his legs, and now in your old age you have no one to help you. Now you are poorer than ever."

The old man spoke again. "You people are obsessed with judging. Don't go so far. Say only that my son broke his legs. Who knows if it is a blessing or a curse? No one knows. We only have a fragment. Life comes in fragments."

It so happened that a few weeks later the country engaged in war against a neighboring country. All the young men of the village were required to join the army. Only the son of the old man was excluded, because he was injured. Once again the people gathered around the old man, crying and screaming because their sons had been taken. There was little chance that they would return. The enemy was strong, and the war would be a losing struggle. They would never see their sons again.

"You were right, old man," they wept. "God knows you were right. This proves it. Your son's accident was a blessing. His legs may be broken, but at least he is with you. Our sons are gone forever."

The old man spoke again. "It is impossible to talk with you. You always draw conclusions. No one knows. Say only this: your sons had to go to war, and mine did not. No one knows if it is a blessing or a curse. No one is wise enough to know. Only God knows."

The old man was right. We only have a fragment. Life's mishaps and horrors are only a page out of a grand book. We must be slow about drawing conclusions. We must reserve judgment on life's storms until we know the whole story.

I don't know where the woodcutter learned his patience. Perhaps from another woodcutter in Galilee. For it was the Carpenter who said it best: "Do not worry about tomorrow, for tomorrow will worry about itself."[3]

He should know. He is the Guide on our journey and the Author of our story. And he has already charted the course and written the final chapter.

chapter nineteen

Chronicle What Christ Has Done

*And we all . . . are being transformed into
his image with ever-increasing glory.*
—2 CORINTHIANS 3:18

Welcome to the "Begin Again Museum of Art." A gallery of people who found a fresh start. A ward of restored hope. A forest of renewed dreams.

An exhibition of second chances.

Wouldn't it be incredible to visit a real one? Wouldn't it be great to walk through such a collection? What if you could see portrayal after portrayal of God meeting people at their greatest points of need and helping them begin again? Not just biblical characters, but contemporary folks just like you? People from your generation and your world!

And what if this gallery contained not only their stories but yours and mine as well? What if there was a place where we could display our "before the beginning" and "after the beginning" experiences? Well, there might be one. I have an idea for such a gallery. It may sound far-fetched, but it's worth sharing.

Before I do, we need to discuss one final question. A crucial question. The Bible contains one story after another of God leading people out of their desperate situations. Tell me, why are these stories in the Bible? Why are the Gospels full of such people? Such hopeless people? Though their situations vary, their conditions don't. They are trapped. Estranged. Rejected. They have nowhere to turn. On their lips a desperate prayer. In their hearts desolate dreams. Before their eyes a dead end.

Again I ask. Why are these portraits in the Bible? Why does this gallery exist? Why did God leave us one tale after another of hopes restored and dreams renewed? So we could be grateful for the past? So we could look back with amazement at what Jesus did?

No. No. No. A thousand times *no.* The purpose of these stories is not to tell us what Jesus *did.* Their purpose is to tell us what Jesus *does.*

"Everything that was written in the past was written to teach us," Paul penned. "The Scriptures give us patience and encouragement so that we can have hope" (Rom. 15:4 NCV).

These are not just Sunday school stories. Not romantic fables. Not somewhere-over-the-rainbow illusions. They are historic moments in which a real God met real pain so we could answer the question, "Where is God when I hurt?"

How does God react to dashed hopes? Read the story of Jairus. How does the Father feel about those who are ill? Stand with him at the pool of Bethesda. Do you long for God to speak to your shattered dreams? Then listen as he speaks to the Emmaus-bound disciples. What is God's word for the shameful? Watch as his finger draws in the dirt of the Jerusalem courtyard.

He's not doing it just for them. He's doing it for me. He's doing it for you.

Which takes us to an empty wall in the gallery—a place reserved for your portraits. One day you will have finished your journey. Now imagine you pick up the brush. Stand in front of the canvases that bear your name and draw your portraits.

It doesn't have to be on a canvas with paint. It could be on paper with a pencil, on a computer with words, in a sculpture with clay, in a song with lyrics. It doesn't matter how you do it, but I urge you to do it. Record your drama. Retell your saga. Revisit your journey.

Begin with "before" your new beginning. What was it like then? Do you remember? Could be decades ago. Perhaps it was yesterday. Maybe you knew Jesus then. Maybe you'd never met him. Again, that doesn't matter. What matters is that you never forget what life was like before you began again.

Remembering can hurt. Parts of our past are not pleasant to revisit. But the recollection is necessary. "Look at what you were when God called you," Paul instructed (1 Cor. 1:26 NCV). We, the adopted, can't forget what life was like as orphans. We, the liberated, should revisit the prison. We, the found, can't forget the despair of being lost.

Amnesia fosters arrogance. We can't afford to forget. We need to remember.

And we need to share our story. Not with everyone but with someone. There is someone who is like you were. And he or she needs to know that God can help him begin again and meet her needs along the journey. Your honest portrayal of your past may inspire the courage for another's future.

But don't just portray the past; depict the present. Describe his touch.

Display the difference he has made in your life. This task has its challenges too. Whereas painting the "before" can be painful, painting the "present" can be unclear. He's not finished with you yet!

So chronicle what Christ has done. If he has brought peace, sketch a dove. If joy, splash a rainbow on a wall. If courage, sing a song about mountain movers. And when you're finished, don't hide it. Put it where you can see it. Put it where you can be reminded daily of the Father's tender power.

And when we all get home, we'll make a gallery.

That's my idea. I know it's crazy, but what if when we all get home, we make a gallery? I don't know if they allow this kind of stuff in heaven. But something tells me the Father won't mind. After all, there's plenty of space and lots of time.

And what an icebreaker! What a way to make friends! Can you envision it? There's Jonah with a life-size whale. Moses is standing in front of a blazing bush. David is giving slingshot lessons. Gideon is letting people touch the fleece—*the* fleece, and Abraham is describing a painting entitled *The Night with a Thousand Stars*.

You can sit with Zacchaeus in his tree. A young boy shows you a basket of five loaves and two fishes. Martha welcomes you into her kitchen. The centurion invites you to touch the cross.

Martin Luther is there with the book of Romans. Susanna Wesley tells how she prayed for her sons—Charles and John. Dwight Moody tells of the day he left the shoe store to preach. And John Newton volunteers to sing "Amazing Grace" with an angelic backup.

Some are famous, most are not . . . but all are heroes. A soldier lets you sit in a foxhole modeled after the one he was in when he met Christ. A housewife shows you her tear-stained New Testament. Beside a Nigerian is the missionary who taught him. And behind a Brazilian is a drawing of the river in which he was baptized.

And somewhere in the midst of this arena of hope is a narrative of your journey. Person after person comes. They listen as if they have all the time in the world. (And they do!) They treat you as if you are royalty. (For you are!) Solomon asks you questions. Job compliments your stamina. Joshua lauds your courage. And when they all applaud, you applaud too. For in heaven everyone knows that all praise goes to one Source.

Please remember, the goal of these stories is not to help us look back with amazement but forward with faith. The God who spoke still speaks. The God who forgave still forgives. The God who came still comes. He comes into our world. He comes into your world. He comes to do what you can't. He comes to help you begin again—to have a second chance in becoming more and more like him as you are changed into his glorious image.

chapter twenty

Listen for the Song of the Whip-poor-will

*No one has ever imagined what God has
prepared for those who love him.*
—1 CORINTHIANS 2:9 NCV

There dwells inside you, deep within, a tiny whip-poor-will. Listen. You will hear him sing. His aria mourns the dusk. His solo signals the dawn.

It is the song of the whip-poor-will.

He will not be silent until the sun is seen.

We forget he is there, so easy is he to ignore. Other animals of the heart are larger, noisier, more demanding, more imposing.

But none is so constant.

Other creatures of the soul are more quickly fed. More simply satisfied. We feed the lion that growls for power. We stroke the tiger that demands affection. We bridle the stallion that bucks control.

But what do we do with the whip-poor-will that yearns for eternity?

For that is his song. That is his task. Out of the gray he sings a golden song. Perched in time he chirps a timeless verse. Peering through pain's shroud, he sees a painless place. Of that place he sings.

And though we try to ignore him, we cannot. His song is ours. Our heart song won't be silenced until we see the dawn.

"God has planted eternity in the hearts of men" (Eccl. 3:11 TLB), says the wise man. But it doesn't take a wise person to know that people long for more than earth. When we see pain, we yearn. When we see hunger, we question why. Senseless deaths. Endless tears. Needless loss. Where do they come from? Where will they lead?

Isn't there more to life than death?

And so sings the whip-poor-will.

We try to quiet this terrible, tiny voice. Like a parent hushing a child, we place a finger over puckered lips and request silence. *I'm too busy now to talk. I'm too busy to think. I'm too busy to question.*

And so we busy ourselves with the task of staying busy.

But occasionally we hear his song. And occasionally we let the song whisper to us that there is something more. There *must* be something more.

And as long as we hear the song, we are comforted. As long as we are discontent, we will search. As long as we know there is a far-off country, we will have hope.

The only ultimate disaster that can befall us, I have come to realize, is to feel ourselves to be at home on earth. As long as we are aliens, we cannot forget our true homeland.[1]

Unhappiness on earth cultivates a hunger for heaven. By gracing us with a deep dissatisfaction, God holds our attention. The only tragedy, then, is to be satisfied prematurely. To settle for earth. To be content in a strange land. To intermarry with the Babylonians and forget Jerusalem.

We are not happy here because we are not at home here because we are "like foreigners and strangers in this world" (1 Peter 2:11 NCV).

Take a fish and place him on the beach.[2] Watch his gills gasp and scales dry. Is he happy? No! How do you make him happy? Do you cover him with a mountain of cash? Do you get him a beach chair and sunglasses? Do you bring him a *Playfish* magazine and martini? Do you wardrobe him in double-breasted fins and people-skinned shoes?

Of course not. Then how do you make him happy? You put him back in his element. You put him back in the water. He will never be happy on the beach, simply because he was not made for the beach.

And you will never be completely happy on earth, simply because you were not made for earth. Oh, you will have moments of joy. You will catch glimpses of light. You will know moments or even days of peace. But they simply do not compare with the happiness that lies ahead.

Thou hast made us for thyself and our hearts are restless until they rest in thee.[3]

Rest on this earth is a false rest. Beware of those who urge you to find happiness here; you won't find it. Guard against the false physicians who promise that joy is only a diet away, a marriage away, a job away, or a transfer away. The prophet denounced people like this: "They tried to heal my people's serious injuries as if they were small wounds. They said, 'It's all right, it's all right.' But really, it is not all right" (Jer. 6:14 NCV).

And it won't be all right until we get home.

Again, we have our moments. The newborn on our breast, the bride on our arm, the sunshine on our back. But even those moments are simply slivers of light breaking through heaven's window. God flirts with us. He tantalizes us. He romances us. Those moments are appetizers for the dish that is to come.

"No one has ever imagined what God has prepared for those who love him" (1 Cor. 2:9 NCV).

What a breathtaking verse! Do you see what it says? *Heaven is beyond our imagination.* We cannot envision it. At our most creative moment, at our deepest thought, at our highest level, we still cannot fathom eternity.

Try this. Imagine a perfect world. Whatever that means to you, imagine it. Does that mean peace? Then envision absolute tranquility. Does a perfect world imply joy? Then create your highest happiness. Will a perfect world have love? If so, ponder a place where love has no bounds. Whatever heaven means to you, imagine it. Get it firmly fixed in your mind. Delight in it. Dream about it. Long for it.

And then smile as the Father reminds you, *No one has ever imagined what God has prepared for those who love him.*

Anything you imagine is inadequate. Anything anyone imagines is inadequate. No one has come close. No one. Think of all the songs about heaven. All the artists' portrayals. All the lessons preached, poems written, and chapters drafted.

When it comes to describing heaven, we are all happy failures.

It's beyond us.

But it's also within us. The song of the whip-poor-will. Let her sing. Let her sing in the dark. Let her sing at the dawn. Let her song remind you that you were not made for this place and that there is a place made just for you.

But until then be realistic. Lower your expectations of earth. This is not heaven, so don't expect it to be. There will never be a newscast with no bad news. There will never be a church with no gossip or competition. There will never be a new car, new wife, or new baby who can give you the joy your heart craves. Only God can.

And God will. Be patient. And be listening. Listening for the song of the whip-poor-will.

A Final Word

I sincerely hope this book has been an inspiration to you. I pray that the pages have worked together to bring this assuring message: God loves you. He is ever available to help you begin again. Before we part company, might I have just another few minutes to discuss God's grand plan for you?

He tailored you for more than a grave, fitted you for a grander destiny than a casket. You are an eternal being equipped with an eternal soul.

What God gave Adam and Eve, he gave to you and me. A soul. "The LORD God formed a man from the dust of the ground and breathed into his nostrils the breath of life, and the man became a living being" (Gen. 2:7).

You are more than a bipedal ape, a chemical fluke, or an atomic surprise. You bear the very breath of God. "[God] breathed into his nostrils the breath of life, and the man became a living being" (Gen. 2:7).

Our souls distinguish us among God's creation. God did not breathe his breath into the giraffe or the beluga whale. He gave a hump to the camel, but he gave his breath, or a soul, to humanity.

Without a soul Adam was without life. His body was complete yet lifeless until God breathed into it. The soul enabled him to breathe, to move, to think . . . indeed, to live.

Humanism may see you as a coincidence of chromosomes, but God sees you as a steward of his essence. You bear the stamp of God. You think. You love. You create. Like Adam, you have a soul.

And, like Adam, you've used your soul to disobey God.

God gave the charter couple one command: "You must not eat from the tree of the knowledge of good and evil, for when you eat from it you will certainly die" (Gen. 2:17).

Disregard God and pay a fatal price. Disobedience, God warned, leads to death. Not just eventual death, mind you, but immediate death. "*When* you eat from it you will certainly die" (emphasis mine).

Wait a second. Did Adam and Eve die? We know they failed the test. Eve ate the fruit and gave some to Adam, who did the same. They hid from God and were banished from the garden. They lived many more years. How do we explain their longevity? Did God change his mind? Or do we misunderstand the definition of *death*? The culprit is the latter. We assume that *death* means cessation of life. It does, eventually. But the first death means separation from God.

Before Adam and Eve lost the ability to breathe, they forfeited their community with God. They hid from him. His presence stirred panic, not peace. Adam heard God's voice and reacted like a kid caught raiding the pantry: "I was afraid" (3:10). Intimacy with God ceased; separation from God began. The guilty pair was "banished . . . from the Garden of Eden" (v. 23). We've loitered outside the garden ever since.

Sin spawns two fatalities: spiritual and physical. Spiritual death separates our souls from God. Physical death separates the soul from the body.

Adam and Eve experienced the first death when they bit the fruit and the second when they bit the dust. "Dust you are and to dust you will return" (Gen. 3:19).

If Adam had not sinned, he would not have died. But he did, so he died.

As do we. Our sin isolates us from God. Left alone we are "dead in trespasses and sins" (Eph. 2:1 NKJV) and consequently "separated from the life of God" (Eph. 4:18).

Spiritual death—the soul separated from God.

Physical death—the soul separated from the body.

So what do we do?

Jesus invites us to believe that "whoever believes in him shall not perish but have eternal life" (John 3:16).

Christ restores what Adam and Eve lost, in the same order they lost it. He reconnects the soul to God, then the body to the soul.

He restores our souls with God when we believe in him: "You who were far away from God are brought near through the blood of Christ's death" (Eph. 2:13 NCV).

He will rejoin our souls with our bodies upon his second coming. Those who die prior to his return pass immediately to their eternal destinies. We know this because of passages like the one in which John sees in heaven "the souls of all who had been martyred" (Rev. 6:9 NLT). Paul equated residence with God as absence from the body. "We really want to be away from this body and be at home with the Lord" (2 Cor. 5:8 NCV). In the era between our deaths and Christ's return, our souls are separated from the flesh. But when Christ comes, "all who are in their graves will hear his voice and come out—those who have done what is good will rise to live, and those who have done what is evil will rise to be condemned" (John 5:28–29).

But how do we know this will happen? Why trust this as a truth? What gives credence to this claim of Christ's?

The empty tomb does. "Since we believe that Jesus died and was raised to life again, we also believe that when Jesus returns, God will bring back with him the believers who have died" (1 Thess. 4:14 NLT).

When Jesus vacated the tomb, he robbed it of its power. Death may touch us, but it cannot have us.

A family was on a picnic when a bumblebee flew near the table. The mother jumped up to shoo it away from her son. He was allergic to bees. He could die if stung. The insect avoided her and flew even closer to the boy. The father stood up and stepped over. Quick-thinking, and quick-handed, he snatched the bee out the air.

After a moment, with a grimace on his face, the dad let the bee go. The boy became upset and ran from the table. The dad calmed him, saying, "Don't worry, Son. You don't have to be afraid."

The father showed his son the palm of his hand that was beginning to swell, and he revealed the stinger. "It's okay. Now all he can do is buzz. This is what could have hurt you, but I took the sting away."

So did Jesus. That's why Paul could ask, "Where, O death, is your victory? Where, O death, is your sting? The sting of death is sin, and the power of sin is the law. But thanks be to God! He gives us the victory through our Lord Jesus Christ" (1 Cor. 15:55–57).

Because of Christ's resurrection, all death can do is buzz.

Trust him, won't you?

Trust him to take your life and turn it into a life worthy of heaven. Thanks to him, you and I can begin again.

Questions for Reflection

PREPARED BY ANDREA LUCADO

Part 1

Believe Your Trustworthy God

1. Think of an instance when you experienced a new beginning in an area of your life. What was that beginning, and how did it help you start over?

2. What new beginning do you need in your life right now?
   - Is anything holding you back from believing a new beginning is possible? If so, what?
   - How do you hope *Begin Again* will help you with that new beginning?

3. How do we compare to the tree stump Max described on pages 1–3?

4. Second Corinthians 3:18 says, "And we all, with unveiled face, beholding the glory of the Lord, are being transformed into the same image from one degree of glory to another. For this comes from the Lord who is the Spirit" (ESV). Have you experienced being transformed from one degree of glory to another? If so, what did that transformation look like?

5. Referring to this type of transformation, Max says, "Expect to be scrubbed, sanded, and varnished a time or two or ten. But in the end the result will be worth the discomfort. You'll be grateful" (p. 3).

   • How do you feel about that statement? Does it make you nervous, excited, hesitant? Why?

   • Considering your answer to the first part of question 2, are you willing to undergo this type of transformation in order to have a new beginning in that area of your life? Why or why not?

Chapter 1

Trust Your Shepherd

1. Max explains that life often feels like a jungle: "But our jungles are comprised of the thicker thickets of contagious diseases, broken hearts, and empty wallets. Our forests are framed with hospital walls and divorce courts" (p. 7).
   - When was the last time life felt disorienting, confusing, as if you couldn't see your way out? Perhaps you feel that way now.
   - What circumstances prompted these feelings?

2. What does Max say is often the result of feeling lost in our "jungles"? (See p. 7.)

3. When you hear the word *hopelessness*, what do you think of, and why?
   - What areas of your life feel hopeless right now?
   - Max asks, "What would it take to restore your hope? What would you need to reenergize your journey?" (p. 7). How would you answer those questions?

4. What three things does Max suggest we need in order to restore our hope when we're in the jungles of life?
   - Of these three which do you need most right now, and why?
   - How would this restore your hope in the face of a seemingly hopeless situation?

5. When Jesus is our rescuer, we can trust he has the right vision to restore our hope and deliver us from the jungle. Read these reminders from Scripture:

   "Don't shuffle along, eyes to the ground, absorbed with the things right in front of you. Look up, and be alert to what is going on around Christ. . . . See things from *his* perspective" (Col. 3:2 THE MESSAGE).

   "I lift up my eyes to the mountains—
        where does my help come from?
   My help comes from the LORD,
        the Maker of heaven and earth.

   "He will not let your foot slip—
        he who watches over you will not slumber. . . .

   "The LORD watches over you . . .
   the sun will not harm you by day,
        nor the moon by night.

   "The LORD will keep you from all harm—
        he will watch over your life." (Ps. 121:1–7)

- According to these passages, where should we focus our gaze?
- Where should it not be?
- Write down everything the Lord will do, according to Psalm 121:1–7.
- How could these promises restore your hope today?

Chapter 2

Give Your Fears
to Your Father

1. The description of Jesus in the Garden of Gethsemane the night
   before his crucifixion is painful to imagine. These verses give us a
   clear sense of Jesus' suffering:

   "He began to be troubled and deeply distressed. Then He
   said to them, 'My soul is exceedingly sorrowful, even to
   death. Stay here and watch.' He went a little farther, and fell
   on the ground, and prayed that if it were possible, the hour
   might pass from Him" (Mark 14:33–35 NKJV).

   "And being in agony, He prayed more earnestly. Then His
   sweat became like great drops of blood falling down to the
   ground" (Luke 22:44 NKJV).

   • In your own words describe how Jesus must have felt.

- How does this image of Jesus differ from other images we have of him in the Gospels or from the way you typically imagine him?
- What did Max say we should do with this image of Jesus? (See p. 7.)
- Though no human pain could truly equal the suffering of Jesus, describe a time you felt an extreme level of fear. What happened? How did you react physically, emotionally?

2. Fill in the blank: "The first one to hear his fear is his _____" (p. 13).
   - Who is typically the first one to hear your fear, and why?
   - Do you typically take your fears to God? Why or why not?

3. Jesus was specific when he said, "Take away this cup of suffering" (Luke 22:42 NCV). Max encourages us to be equally precise when we take our fears to God. What specific fear do you need to pray about right now?

4. In Psalm 23:4 David wrote, "Even though I walk through the darkest valley, I will fear no evil, for you are with me; your rod and your staff, they comfort me."
   - Why was David able to say he would fear no evil?
   - How could you find comfort in God today as David did in this passage?

Chapter 3

Seeing with Eyes Closed

1. According to this chapter what blind spot do we all have? (See p. 16.)

   - How do you personally cope with an unknown future? Do you try to guess what will happen? Do you avoid thinking about it or obsess over it? Explain your answer.

   - Is there an unknown in your life that is causing fear or anxiety? If so, what is that unknown, and why is it causing you unrest?

2. Although Jairus was the leader of the synagogue and held a prominent place in his community, when his daughter fell ill, how did he approach Jesus in Mark 5:23?

   - Have you ever felt this way—as Max describes it, "when everything you have to offer is nothing compared to what you are asking to receive" (p. 18)? If so, describe the situation.

- What were you pleading for?
- Whom did you plead with—God, Jesus, a friend, someone else?

3. How might Jairus have felt when he was told, "Your daughter is dead. There is no need to bother the teacher anymore" (Mark 5:35 ncv)?
    - Have you ever been given a hopeless message? How did you respond?
    - What was Jesus' response in Mark 5:36? Why might he have responded as he did?

4. Jesus ignored the voices telling him Jairus's daughter was already dead. Have you ever struggled with the voices of those around you saying that your situation was hopeless? If so, how did those voices affect you?

5. Jesus told Jairus, "Don't be afraid; just believe" (v. 36). What would change if you heeded Jesus' words even as the voices around you are encouraging otherwise?
    - What do you need to believe in today?
    - What do you not want to fear anymore?
    - Max says, "When tragedy strikes, we, too, are left to choose what we see. We can see either the hurt or the Healer" (p. 19). What do you typically choose to see, or what are you choosing to see right now in a difficult unknown?

6. What did Jesus do with the people who were claiming Jairus's daughter was dead? (See v. 40.)
    - What voices do you need to throw out today?
    - How could Jesus help you do this?

Chapter 4

Don't Give Up

1. Name a failure in your life. If this is a recent failure, how did it feel to fail? If this is a failure in your past, how do you feel now when you think about this failure?

2. Has any failure—past or present—led you to believe you can't begin again in an area of your life? What are the consequences of not beginning again in that area? What might be possible if you did begin again in that area?

3. Scripture is full of stories of people who failed God and others. Read Luke 15:11–18. How had the prodigal son failed?
   - Does his failure have any similarities with yours? If so, what?
   - What had transpired in the story before he decided, "I will arise and go to my father" (NKJV)?
   - Have you ever had a turning point in your own failure—a

163

moment when you decided to remove yourself from the pigpen of regret and shame and turn to God? If so, how did God respond?

- Are you in a moment of similar need? What would convince you to ask God to help you escape the pigpen of regret and shame? How could you turn to God?

4. Read the rest of the story of the prodigal son in Luke 15:18–24. How did the father respond to his son?

- What does this say about how God responds to us when we turn to him in our pigpen moments?
- What does this say about our failures and new beginnings?

Chapter 5

Follow the God Who Follows You

1. Psalm 23:6 says, "Surely goodness and mercy shall follow me all the days of my life; and I will dwell in the house of the LORD forever" (NKJV). Max breaks down the promises behind key phrases and words in this verse.
   - What does the word *surely* promise us?
   - What does the phrase "goodness and mercy" promise us?
   - What does it mean for God to follow us?
   - Have you ever experienced this persistence from God? If so, how?

2. Max mentions several characters from the Bible whom God pursued. Read more about one of these characters in John 4:1–26.
   - How did Jesus pursue the Samaritan woman with his words and actions?

- How did the woman respond?
- Why do you think Jesus revealed his divine identity to this woman?

3. Max tells the story of Eric, a homeless man whose sister, Debbie, found him near the end of his life. How did Debbie's pursuit of Eric parallel God's pursuit of us?

4. How could trusting that God is pursuing you all the days of your life give you hope for a new beginning today?

Chapter 6

Accept the Gift of Himself

1. What is making you weary right now—a relationship, job, circumstances? Describe this kind of weariness and how it affects your daily life.

2. You could say Job was weary. He experienced every hardship a man could. Read Job 1:13–22 and 2:7–10. What and whom did Job lose in these passages? List them below.

3. Have you ever been through a Job season, where it seemed that everything in your life was in disarray?
   - If so, what was hardest about that season?
   - What hardships did you endure?
   - Did you talk to God during this time? If so, how did you approach him? With anger? Arguments? Pleading? Questions?

4. Job's friends tried to find a reason for his suffering. Eliphaz said, "Remember now, who ever perished being innocent? Or where were the upright ever cut off? Even as I have seen, those who plow iniquity and sow trouble reap the same. By the blast of God they perish, and by the breath of His anger they are consumed" (Job 4:7–9 NKJV).

Bildad said, "How long will you speak these things, and the words of your mouth be like a strong wind? Does God subvert judgment? Or does the Almighty pervert justice? If your sons have sinned against Him, He has cast them away for their transgression. If you would earnestly seek God and make your supplication to the Almighty, if you were pure and upright, surely now He would awake for you, and prosper your rightful dwelling place" (Job 8:2–6 NKJV).

Elihu said, "He will redeem his soul from going down to the Pit, and his life shall see the light. Behold, God works all these things, twice, in fact, three times with a man, to bring back his soul from the Pit, that he may be enlightened with the light of life" (Job 33:28–30 NKJV).

- What was Eliphaz's reasoning for Job's suffering?
- What was Bildad's reasoning?
- What was Elihu's reasoning?
- Do you agree or disagree with what these friends told Job?
- When you are suffering, what questions do you tend to ask God?

5. Now read God's response in Job 38:4–11 to the question of Job's suffering. What does Max say was the purpose of God's questions for Job? (See pp. 47–48.)

- How did these questions and statements from God help Job understand his suffering?

- How could shifting your perspective from questioning God to believing in God's sovereignty help you in times of suffering?

6. Job eventually got an opportunity to begin again. His story ended with hope: "And the LORD restored Job's losses when he prayed for his friends. Indeed the LORD gave Job twice as much as he had before" (Job 42:10 NKJV).
    - Have you ever experienced a new beginning after a dark season of suffering? If so, did your new beginning refine your view of the suffering season? If so, how?
    - How could Job's new beginning bring you hope in whatever season of weariness or suffering you are in today?

Chapter 7

Rely on the Holy Spirit

1. What do you know about the Holy Spirit? What role does the Holy Spirit play in your life, if any?

2. Ephesians 1:13–14 says, "You were sealed in Him with the Holy Spirit of promise, who is given as a pledge of our inheritance" (NASB).
   - What sorts of images does Max connect with the word *sealed*? (See p. 52.)
   - Is there anyone in your life that you feel "sealed" to? Perhaps a spouse, longtime friend, or relative? If so, describe that relationship and how being sealed to this person affects your confidence in that relationship.
   - How could the relationship you just described help you better understand your relationship with the Holy Spirit and his purpose in your life?

3. Read the following verses in Romans.

"The Spirit we received does not make us slaves again to fear; it makes us children of God. With that Spirit we cry out, 'Father.' And the Spirit himself joins with our spirits to say we are God's children" (Rom. 8:15–16 NCV).

"The love of God has been poured out in our hearts by the Holy Spirit who was given to us" (Rom. 5:5 NKJV).

"The Spirit comes to the aid of our weakness. We do not even know how we ought to pray, . . . but through our inarticulate groans the Spirit himself is pleading for us, and God who searches our inmost being knows what the Spirit means, because he pleads for God's own people in God's own way" (Rom. 8:26–27 NEB).

- According to Romans 8:15–16, how does the Holy Spirit affect our identity?
- According to Romans 5:5, how does the Holy Spirit allow us to experience the love of God?
- According to Romans 8:26–27, how does the Holy Spirit help us in prayer and in times of need?

4. After learning more about the Holy Spirit, would you say you use the Spirit's power in your life? Why or why not? How could you use the Spirit today in prayer, for help, or to experience God's love?

Chapter 8

Shelter in His Protection

1. How do you think God sees you? When he considers you, what does he think about? Be honest, and write down whatever comes to mind.
   - What kind of things did you write down—negative, positive, a mix of both?
   - Why do you believe God sees you this way?

2. Max writes, "We assume God cares for the purebreds of the world. The clean-nosed, tidy-living, convent-created souls of society" (p. 58). Have you ever made this assumption about God? Why or why not?

3. Psalm 91:1–6 says:

   "Those who live in the shelter of the Most High
   will find rest in the shadow of the Almighty.
   This I declare about the LORD:

He alone is my refuge, my place of safety;

he is my God, and I trust him.

For he will rescue you from every trap

and protect you from deadly disease.

He will cover you with his feathers.

He will shelter you with his wings.

His faithful promises are your armor and protection.

Do not be afraid of the terrors of the night,

nor the arrow that flies in the day.

Do not dread the disease that stalks in darkness,

nor the disaster that strikes at midday" (NLT).

- How is God described in this passage?
- Based on this passage what does God promise you?
- According to the first two lines, who gets to benefit from these promises?

4. Psalm 91 says those who find shelter in God will be protected from harm. In times of loneliness, fear, or trouble, this beautiful promise is a strong anchor, worthy of memorizing for such times.

- Have you ever felt protected by God in a difficult circumstance in your life? If so, how did this affect your faith?
- On the other hand have you ever felt that God was absent during a difficult time? If so, how did it affect your faith?

5. How does our perspective differ from God's when it comes to the difficulties in our lives? (See p. 61.)

- How does this affect the way you see your circumstances today or a difficulty you may be facing?
- What promises from Psalm 91 do you need to apply to this circumstance? Or how could these promises have been helpful during a difficulty you faced in the past?

Chapter 9

Settle Down Deep in His Love

1. Which person do you believe loves you most in this world? A parent, sibling, partner?
   - Why did you select this person?
   - How do you know this person loves you?
   - How does this person's love for you make you feel?

2. First John 4:16 says, "God is love." What does it mean for God to be not just loving but to be love itself?

3. Regarding Pipín Ferreras, the record-breaking diver, Max says, "Having plunged the equivalent of five stories, where can he turn and not see water? To the right, to the left, beneath him, above him . . . Can a person go equally deep into God's love?" (p. 66).
   - What is your answer to this question?

- Have you felt the depth of God's love in such a way that everywhere you turned, it was there? If so, describe that experience.

4. Read the following verses.

"The LORD did not set his affection on you and choose you because you were more numerous than other peoples, for you were the fewest of all peoples. But it was because the LORD loved you" (Deut. 7:7–8).

"God showed his great love for us by sending Christ to die for us while we were still sinners" (Rom. 5:8 TLB).

"May your roots go down deep into the soil of God's marvelous love; and may you be able to feel and understand, as all God's children should, how long, how wide, how deep, and how high his love really is; and to experience this love for yourselves, though it is so great that you will never see the end of it or fully know or understand it. And so at last you will be filled up with God himself" (Eph. 3:17–19 TLB).

- According to Deuteronomy 7:7–8, why does God love us?
- According to Romans 5:8, what was God's ultimate act of love for us?
- According to Ephesians 3:17–19, what is the nature of God's love?
- Look back at your answer to question 1. According to these verses how is God's love different from this person's love in your life?

5. Spend some time reading Ephesians 3:17–19 again. Personalize the passage by replacing "you" and "your" and "yourselves" with "I" and "my" and "myself." How could this assurance of God's love help you as you go about your day and week?

Chapter 10

Hold On to Your Soul Anchor

1. Is there anything in your life—a person, a circumstance, a relationship—that you have lost hope in? If so, why? When was the last time you felt hopeful about this situation?

2. Hebrews 6:19–20 says, "We have this hope as an anchor for the soul, firm and secure. It enters the inner sanctuary behind the curtain, where our forerunner, Jesus, has entered on our behalf."
   - What is the purpose of an anchor?
   - How can hope be an anchor in our lives?
   - More specifically how is Jesus our hope and anchor?

3. Max tells the story of Jonathan McComb, who tragically lost his family in a flood. Yet during his family's funeral Jonathan preached a message of hope. Have you ever experienced hope during a

179

seemingly hopeless time? If so, what gave you hope, and how did it help you persevere through this "hopeless" time?

4. Romans 15:13 says, "Now may the God of hope fill you with all joy and peace in believing, that you may abound in hope by the power of the Holy Spirit" (NKJV).
   - What is significant about the word *abound* in this passage?
   - How would your daily life change if you were abounding in hope in God?

5. Max asks, "Is what I'm hooked to stronger than what I'll go through?" (p. 83).
   - How would you answer that question today?
   - Does your answer give you more or less hope regarding the situation you described in question 1?

6. Max says, "People of the new beginning make daily decisions to secure their anchors in the promises of God" (pp. 83–84). He suggests remembering these promises by writing them down. Spend some time writing down any promises you've read in Scripture or promises you feel the Lord has given you. Reflect on how the assurance of these promises makes you feel and how they could give you hope today.

Chapter 11

Choose Faith

1. It is one thing to know the promises God has made. It is another to believe he will keep them. Based on your experience and relationship with God at this point in your life, do you believe he keeps his promises? Why or why not? It's okay if your answer is not a simple yes or no. Explain where you would place yourself on the spectrum today.

2. Read some of the promises below that God has made in Scripture.

   "Weeping may stay for the night,
          but rejoicing comes in the morning" (Ps. 30:5).

   "The righteous person may have many troubles,
          but the LORD delivers him from them all" (Ps. 34:19).

"The LORD sustains them on their sickbed
>   and restores them from their bed of illness" (Ps. 41:3).

"When you pass through the waters,
>   I will be with you" (Isa. 43:2).

"In my Father's house are many rooms. . . . I go to prepare a place for you" (John 14:2 ESV).

"My grace is sufficient for you" (2 Cor. 12:9).

- Which of these promises do you most need today, and why?
- Which promise is easiest for you to believe, and why?
- Which promise is hardest for you to believe, and why? What would you need to believe about God in order to believe this promise?

3. Max asks an important question when it comes to trusting God's promises: "Does God's integrity make a difference?" (p. 89).
   - How would you answer this question?
   - What do you believe about God's integrity, and why?
   - Max gave an example of trusting in his pilot's integrity when the pilot told the passengers their planes wouldn't leave without them. In your life who has great integrity?
   - How does this affect your trust in this person's words?

4. Max refers to a man who had lost his twenty-four-year-old daughter but still clung to the promises of God. The man said, "Faith is a choice" (p. 88).

- What do you think about this statement? Do you agree or disagree? Why?
- Have you ever had to choose faith? If so, how did choosing faith affect your circumstances or your attitude toward those circumstances?
- Is there an area of your life right now in which you feel you need to choose faith? If so, what could it look like to choose faith today?

Chapter 12

Let Your Father Fight for You

1. Hebrews 13:5–6 says, "For [God] has said, 'I will never leave you or forsake you.' So we can say with confidence, 'The Lord is my helper; I will not be afraid. What can anyone do to me?'" (NRSV).
   - What do you fear that someone else can or will do to you?
   - How does this fear affect your life?
   - How does it affect your faith in God and his protection?

2. Max points out that the Greek word for *helper* in Hebrews 13:6 is *boēthos*.
   - What is the significance of this word? (See p. 95.)
   - How does knowing this definition help you understand how God protects you?

3. We often think of God as someone who loves us, knows us, or directs our path, but do you often think of God as someone who fights for you? Why or why not?

4. This image of God fighting on our behalf is depicted often in the Old Testament. Read the following verses.

   "Be strong and courageous; do not be afraid nor dismayed before the king of Assyria, nor before all the multitude that is with him; for there are more with us than with him. With him is an arm of flesh; but with us is the LORD our God, to help us and to fight our battles" (2 Chron. 32:7–8 NKJV).

   "Plead my cause, O LORD, with those who strive with me;
   Fight against those who fight against me.
   Take hold of shield and buckler,
   And stand up for my help" (Ps. 35:1–2 NKJV).

   - According to 2 Chronicles 32:7–8 what was the difference between Israel's army and Assyria's?
   - Is someone fighting against you right now? If so, how have you responded to that fight?
   - "What do you think would happen if you did what the psalmist did in Psalm 35 and asked God to fight against those who fight against you, rather than taking on the fight yourself?"

5. Perhaps the ultimate proof that God fights for us can be seen on the cross when Jesus fought sin on our behalf and was victorious.

- How can the promise that you have been saved for eternity bring perspective to what you fear today?
- How can this promise increase your faith and trust in God's protection?

Chapter 13

Keep Believing God's Promise

1. Read Matthew 1:1–6, 16 below.

"The book of the genealogy of Jesus Christ, the Son of David, the Son of Abraham:

"Abraham begot Isaac, Isaac begot Jacob, and Jacob begot Judah and his brothers. Judah begot Perez and Zerah by Tamar, Perez begot Hezron, and Hezron begot Ram. Ram begot Amminadab, Amminadab begot Nahshon, and Nahshon begot Salmon. Salmon begot Boaz by Rahab, Boaz begot Obed by Ruth, Obed begot Jesse, and Jesse begot David the king. . . .

"And Jacob begot Joseph the husband of Mary, of whom was born Jesus who is called Christ" (NKJV).

- Why did Matthew begin his gospel this way? (See pp. 100–102.)

- Underline the names of people in this passage who had a tainted past. Why did Jesus' lineage include characters like these?

2. When you think about your past, what do you focus on and feel—mistakes, regrets, happy memories, heartache, love?
   - How does your past affect your present?
   - How does your past affect the way you relate to God?

3. What significance or promise does Jesus' name bring to his lineage?
   - How could Jesus redeem the way you feel about your own history?
   - How could the promise of Christ help you begin again despite a spotted past?

4. Matthew 24:13 says, "But he who endures to the end shall be saved" (NKJV). Do you feel that your faith endurance right now is strong, weak, or somewhere in between?
   - Note that the verse doesn't say "he who has an ironclad faith" or "he who never waivers in his faith." It simply says "he who endures." What does that say to you?
   - How could this idea of endurance give you hope in your own faith journey?

5. Of the promises you studied in this section, which one stands out the most to you, and why?
   - What promises of God do you need to cling to in order to endure to the end?
   - What promises of God do you need to remember to simply endure today?

Chapter 14

Be You

1. Max opens this chapter by saying, "No one else has your 'you-ness'" (p. 107). How would you describe your you-ness? What makes you *you*? Is this an easy or difficult question for you to consider, and why?

2. Scripture has quite a bit to say about the way God created us individually. Read Psalm 139:13–18 below.

   "For you created my inmost being;
   you knit me together in my mother's womb.
   I praise you because I am fearfully and wonderfully made;
       your works are wonderful,
       I know that full well.
   My frame was not hidden from you
       when I was made in the secret place,
       when I was woven together in the depths of the earth.

Your eyes saw my unformed body;

>all the days ordained for me were written in your book
>
>before one of them came to be.

How precious to me are your thoughts, God!

>How vast is the sum of them!

Were I to count them,

>they would outnumber the grains of sand—
>
>when I awake, I am still with you."

- What does this passage say about how God created you?
- What does it say about how God feels about you?
- What does it say about who you are and your unique qualities?
- Considering what makes you *you*, what are some special qualities you imagine God thought of as he created you?

3. Although Scripture encourages it, being yourself in a culture marked by comparison and competition is not easy. Do you feel as though you are generally able to be yourself in your work environment, in your relationships, in your faith? Why or why not?

- Perhaps you feel as though you can be yourself in some situations but not others. What makes the difference?
- In what situations is it easier to be yourself?
- In what situations is it more difficult to be yourself?

4. We are unique in personality, and we are also unique in our gifts and occupations and what we can bring to the world because of them. Read 1 Corinthians 12:4–11:

"God's various gifts are handed out everywhere; but they all originate in God's Spirit. God's various ministries are carried out everywhere; but they all originate in God's Spirit. God's various expressions of power are in action everywhere; but God himself is behind it all. Each person is given something to do that shows who God is: Everyone gets in on it, everyone benefits. All kinds of things are handed out by the Spirit, and to all kinds of people! The variety is wonderful" (THE MESSAGE).

- According to this passage where does God hand out his gifts?
- What is the purpose of these gifts?
- What would you say are your God-given gifts?
- Which of those gifts are you actively using today?

5. How does comparison steal our sense of worth and value?
    - Do you ever fall prey to the comparison trap? If so, whom do you typically compare yourself to, and why?
    - How do you feel about yourself after you have compared yourself—your looks, your accomplishments, your talent, etc.—to someone else?
    - What do you think would change if you stopped comparing yourself to others? How would it affect your thoughts, what you do, how you view others, and how you view yourself?

Chapter 15

Share What God Has Given

1. Max tells a powerful story about childhood friends Arthur and Skinner. Based on this story how do you think Arthur felt about his friend Skinner? What makes you think this?

   • Is there anyone in your life you feel this way about—someone for whom you would sacrifice anything? If so, who is this person, and why do you feel this way about him or her?

   • Think of an instance when someone made a significant sacrifice for you. Explain what happened and how the sacrifice affected your relationship. Have you made a significant sacrifice for someone else? How did that sacrifice change you personally?

2. The parable of the prodigal son tells the story of a rebellious son who squandered his inheritance and then sheepishly returned to

his father's household. You've already read part of the story. Now read the complete text of Luke 15:21–24 below.

"The son said to him, 'Father, I have sinned against heaven and against you. I am no longer worthy to be called your son.' "But the father said to his servants, 'Quick! Bring the best robe and put it on him. Put a ring on his finger and sandals on his feet. Bring the fattened calf and kill it. Let's have a feast and celebrate. For this son of mine was dead and is alive again; he was lost and is found.' So they began to celebrate."

- What is the historical significance of the ring in this passage? (See p. 115.)
- Max asks, "Would you have given this prodigal son power-of-attorney privileges over your affairs? Would you have entrusted him with a credit card? Would you have given him this ring?" (p. 115). How would you answer these questions?
- Considering your answers above, how does it make you feel to be God's ambassador?
- Do you believe you've been a good ambassador for God? Why or why not?

3. We are called not only to receive God in our own lives but to share him with others. How does Max suggest we do this? (See pp. 116–117.)
    - Has anyone ever showed up for you in a time of need? If so, who was it, and how did that person show up?
    - How did this person's presence change your circumstances or your perspective during this time?

4. Our words can be a powerful way to show up for others. Read the following passages.

"Do not let any unwholesome talk come out of your mouths, but only what is helpful for building others up according to their needs, that it may benefit those who listen" (Eph. 4:29).

"For God did not appoint us to suffer wrath but to receive salvation through our Lord Jesus Christ. He died for us so that, whether we are awake or asleep, we may live together with him. Therefore encourage one another and build each other up, just as in fact you are doing" (1 Thess. 5:9–11).

- According to Ephesians 4:29, how should we talk to others?
- According to 1 Thessalonians 5:9–11, why do we encourage and build up each other?
- How could you use your words today to encourage the people in your life and be an ambassador for God?

Chapter 16

Love Those in Need

1. Fill in the blank: "When we love those in need, we are loving
   _____" (p. 121). What does this mean to you? Is it confusing or
   enlightening? Explain your response.

2. When was the last time you helped someone in need?
   - What did you do, and how did it make you feel?
   - When was the last time someone helped you?
   - How did this person's help make you feel?

3. Read part of Jesus' final sermon in Matthew 25:34–40 below.

   Then the King will say to those on his right, "Come, you who
   are blessed by my Father; take your inheritance, the kingdom
   prepared for you since the creation of the world. For I was
   hungry and you gave me something to eat, I was thirsty and
   you gave me something to drink, I was a stranger and you

invited me in, I needed clothes and you clothed me, I was sick and you looked after me, I was in prison and you came to visit me."

Then the righteous will answer him, "Lord, when did we see you hungry and feed you, or thirsty and give you something to drink? When did we see you a stranger and invite you in, or needing clothes and clothe you? When did we see you sick or in prison and go to visit you?"

The King will reply, "Truly I tell you, whatever you did for one of the least of these brothers and sisters of mine, you did for me."

- What do those who are blessed by the Father receive?
- Who is considered blessed?
- Based on this sermon how important to God is our treatment of others?
- Does this change your perspective or motivation about doing good for your neighbor? Why or why not?

4. According to Max what is the connection between compassion and salvation? Do you agree or disagree with his thoughts, and why?

5. Not all of us are called to be a Mother Teresa. But as Max said, "None of us can help everyone. But all of us can help someone" (p. 124).
    - Who do you know that needs help today?
    - How could you help this person in a way that would display the love of Christ?

Chapter 17

Make a Difference

1. Max told a story about a sea captain who was looking for Father Benjamin. What point does this story make about the impact we can have on others?

2. What would you need to do in your life to say confidently, "I have fought the good fight, I have finished the race, I have kept the faith" (2 Tim. 4:7)?
   - How are you currently using the gifts God has given you? Can you think of additional ways to use your gifts?
   - How could you share those gifts with others in a way that they would know the love of God?
   - How could you help those in need around you?

3. When the captain asked the island residents where Father Benjamin was, they showed him the mark Father Benjamin had left on their

lives: a clinic, fishponds, a chapel, and a Bible. Were someone to look for you after you died, what would your neighbors show this person to prove the impact you left on that world?

Chapter 18

Reserve Judgment of Life's Storms

1. Have you ever judged an experience in your life to be either good or bad and then the opposite turned out to be true? If so, what was that experience, and what did you learn from it? Why do you think you jumped to conclusions about this event?

2. First Corinthians 13:9–12 says, "For we know in part and we prophesy in part, but when completeness comes, what is in part disappears. When I was a child, I talked like a child, I thought like a child, I reasoned like a child. When I became a man, I put the ways of childhood behind me. For now we see only a reflection as in a mirror; then we shall see face to face. Now I know in part; then I shall know fully, even as I am fully known."

   • What do you think Paul is referring to when he says, "when completeness comes"?

- Give an example of something you understood in childhood but that you understand differently now. What allowed you to see this in a new way?
- Identify something you believed about God or your faith when you were younger that has changed as you've gotten older.
- What is something you have limited knowledge of now ("a reflection as in a mirror") that you wish you understood better?

3. Max shares a story of a woodcutter and his neighbors.
   - How did the woodcutter's neighbors respond when his prize horse was stolen?
   - How did they respond when the horse returned with a dozen other horses?
   - How did they respond when the woodcutter's son broke his legs?
   - How did they respond when the woodcutter's son was spared from going to war?
   - How did the woodcutter respond to his neighbors' judgments, and why did he respond this way?
   - When unforeseen events happen in your life, how do you tend to respond? Do you judge them as the woodcutter's neighbors did, or do you reserve judgment as the woodcutter did? Why do you respond this way?

4. What event or circumstance in your life do you not fully understand right now?
   - What are your questions about this situation?

- How is this affecting your faith or your relationship with God?
- Read 1 Corinthians 13:9–12 again. Does that passage bring clarity or hope to this event or circumstance? If so, which part, and why?

Chapter 19

Chronicle What Christ Has Done

1. Believing in Christ is a soul rebirth. When you met Christ, you effectively began again, everything in the past, now past. If you were ever given a second chance, you know what it's like to begin again. If you were ever rescued from a desperate situation and had your hope restored, you know what it's like to begin again. Do you remember what you were like before this new beginning? Do you remember what was different in your life? Write as much as you can remember about this "before" time.

2. What is the purpose of remembering who we were and what we were like before we had a begin-again experience? Even if it is painful for you to recollect some of those memories, why is it important to remember anyway?

3. Max talked about a number of biblical characters in this book—some who listened to God and succeeded, others who didn't and failed, and many who fell somewhere in between, but they all encountered God. As Max said, "The Bible contains one story after another of God leading people out of their desperate situations. Tell me, why are these stories in the Bible? Why are the Gospels full of such people?" (p. 138). How would you answer those questions? How do these characters' stories give you hope?

4. Paul said to the church at Corinth, "Brothers and sisters, think of what you were when you were called. Not many of you were wise by human standards; not many were influential; not many were of noble birth" (1 Cor. 1:26).

    • What were you when you were called?
    • How have you changed since then?
    • What has God used in your life for good?
    • What has God freed you from?

5. Max talks about a potential heavenly scenario in which we get to hear each other's stories of beginning again—from Jonah, to Zacchaeus, to Martin Luther, to King David, to you. How would you tell your story?

Chapter 20

Listen for the Song of the Whip-poor-will

1. Beginning again can be difficult in a world full of heartbreak, pain, and unknowns. This is why Max encourages us to listen to the whip-poor-will. What does the whip-poor-will represent?
   - Would you say you've heard his song in your soul before?
   - If so, how do you experience this yearning for eternity?

2. Read Ecclesiastes 3:1–11:

   There is a time for everything,

   and a season for every activity under the heavens:
   a time to be born and a time to die,
   a time to plant and a time to uproot,
   a time to kill and a time to heal,

a time to tear down and a time to build,

a time to weep and a time to laugh,

a time to mourn and a time to dance,

a time to scatter stones and a time to gather them,

a time to embrace and a time to refrain from embracing,

a time to search and a time to give up,

a time to keep and a time to throw away,

a time to tear and a time to mend,

a time to be silent and a time to speak,

a time to love and a time to hate,

a time for war and a time for peace.

What do workers gain from their toil? I have seen the burden God has laid on the human race. He has made everything beautiful in its time. He has also set eternity in the human heart; yet no one can fathom what God has done from beginning to end.

- Why do you think this passage talks about God's perfect timing on earth as well as keeping eternity in mind? How might these ideas work together?
- What kind of seasons have you experienced in your life? What kind of season are you in right now?
- Have you experienced any of the "times" mentioned in this passage? If so, which ones?
- Is it helpful for you to think of these times as seasons? Why or why not?
- How might it help to keep eternity in mind as you go through the seasons of life?

3. Peter wrote a letter to a group of early Christians who were exiles, scattered among several different provinces: Pontus, Galatia, Cappadocia, Asia, and Bithynia (1 Peter 1:1). Peter referred to them as "foreigners and strangers in this world" (1 Peter 2:11 NCV).

   • Have you ever felt like a foreigner or stranger in this world? If so, how?

   • How could the promise of eternity with God bring you peace when you feel this way?

4. Someday we will all begin again. In Christ even death is not the end of the story. As Max writes, "Why trust this as a truth? What gives credence to this claim of Christ's? The empty tomb does. 'Since we believe that Jesus died and was raised to life again, we also believe that when Jesus returns, God will bring back with him the believers who have died'" (p. 150).

   • How do you feel about the empty tomb? Do you believe in it, distrust it, or aren't sure? Why?

   • End this time of reflection in prayer. Bring to God any concerns or questions you have about this ultimate new beginning, and ask him how in your life you could begin again today.

Sources

Text adapted and excerpted from the following sources:

Chapter 1: Trust Your Shepherd
Traveling Light

Chapter 2: Give Your Fears to Your Father
Traveling Light

Chapter 3: Seeing with Eyes Closed
He Still Moves Stones

Chapter 4: Don't Give Up
Glory Days

Chapter 5: Follow the God Who Follows You
Traveling Light

Chapter 6: Accept the Gift of Himself
In the Eye of the Storm

Chapter 7: Rely On the Holy Spirit
Come Thirsty

Chapter 8: Shelter in His Protection
Come Thirsty

Chapter 9: Settle Down Deep in His Love
Come Thirsty

Chapter 10: Hold On to Your Soul Anchor
Unshakable Hope

Chapter 11: Choose Faith
Glory Days

Chapter 12: Let Your Father Fight for You
Glory Days

Chapter 13: Keep Believing God's Promise
When God Whispers Your Name

Chapter 14: Be You
Glory Days

Chapter 15: Share What God Has Given

A Love Worth Giving

Chapter 16: Love Those in Need

Outlive Your Life

Chapter 17: Make a Difference

Outlive Your Life

Chapter 18: Reserve Judgment of Life's Storms

In the Eye of the Storm

Chapter 19: Chronicle What Christ Has Done

He Still Moves Stones

Chapter 20: Listen for the Song of the Whip-poor-will

When God Whispers Your Name

Notes

Chapter 4: Don't Give Up

1. Leigh Montville, "Wide and to the Right: The Kick That Will Forever Haunt Scott Norwood," SI.com, September 12, 2011, https://www.si.com /more-sports/2011/09/12/scott-norwoodsuperbowl.

2. "The size of this group is indicated by the text as 30,000 men, which appears to be an unusually large contingent for such a secret maneuver as ambush close to the city. One plausible answer to the problem is that the text should read 'thirty officers.' This suggestion is made by R. E. D. Clark, who points out that the Hebrew word *elep*, translated 'thousand,' can also be translated as 'chief' or 'officer,' as it is translated in other passages (cf. 1 Chron. 12:23–27; 2 Chron. 13:3, 17; 17:14–19). If this were the case, then the thirty-man group was a highly selected commando unit, assigned to enter the vacated city and burn it. This view may better explain also the description of the contingent as chosen for being 'mighty men of valor'— more meaningful to a thirty-man group than to a 30,000-man unit. It should be noted here, however, that the second ambuscade definitely involved 5,000 men (8:12)." Irving L. Jensen, *Joshua: Rest-Land Won* (Chicago: Moody Press, 1966), 72.

Chapter 5: Follow the God Who Follows You

1. F. B. Meyer, *The Shepherd Psalm* (Grand Rapids, MI: Kregel Publications, 1991), 125.
2. This story initially appeared in *The Gift for All People*. Thanks to Multnomah Publishing for allowing us to use it in *Traveling Light and Begin Again*.

Chapter 6: Accept the Gift of Himself

1. Job 13:4–5 TLB.
2. Job 33:29–30.
3. Job 38:2.
4. Job 38:3.
5. Job 38:4 TLB.
6. Job 38:5–7 TLB.
7. Job 38:12–13 TLB.
8. Job 38:17–21 TLB.
9. Job 40:4–5 TLB.
10. Job 41:11 TLB.
11. Job 42:5 TLB.

Chapter 7: Rely On the Holy Spirit

1. William C. Frey, *The Dance of Hope: Finding Ourselves in the Rhythm of God's Great Story* (Colorado Springs, CO: WaterBrook, 2003), 174.

Chapter 9: Settle Down Deep in His Love

1. Gary Smith, "The Rapture of the Deep," *Sports Illustrated*, 16 June 2003, 62–78.
2. David Brainerd, quoted in Cynthia Heald, "Becoming a Friend of God," *Discipleship Journal*, no. 54 (1989): 22.
3. Craig Childs, *The Secret Knowledge of Water: Discovering the Essence of the American Desert* (Boston: Little, Brown, 2000), 61–62.

Part 3

1. Herbert Lockyer, *All the Promises of the Bible* (Grand Rapids: Zondervan, 1962), 10.

Chapter 10: Hold On to Your Soul Anchor

1. Lynda Schultz, "The Story Behind the Song," *Thrive*, www.thrive -magazine.ca/blog/40/.
2. Schultz, "The Story."

Chapter 11: Choose Faith

1. Used with permission.
2. Edward Mote, "This Solid Rock" in *Sacred Selections for the Church: A Collection of Sacred Selections Featuring Choice Favorites Old and New* (Kendallville, IN: Sacred Selections, 1956), no. 120.

Chapter 12: Let Your Father Fight for You

1. Sean Alfano, "Teens Arrested after Posting YouTube Video of Beating 13-Year-Old Boy and Hanging Him from a Tree," *New York Daily News*, February 1, 2011, www.nydailynews.com/news/national/teens-arrested -posting-youtube-video-beating-13-year-old-boy-hanging-tree-article -1.137868. See also Rick Reilly, "Eagles over Wolves in a Rout," ESPN. com, last modified February 14, 2011, http://espn.com/espn/news/story?id =6120346.
2. W. E. Vine, *Vine's Expository Dictionary of New Testament Words: A Comprehensive Dictionary of the Original Greek Words with Their Precise Meanings for English Readers* (McLean, VA: MacDonald Publishing, n.d.), 554.

Chapter 14: Be You

1. Adapted from Joel Osteen, *Every Day a Friday: How to Be Happier 7 Days a Week* (New York: FaithWords, 2011), 131–32.

Chapter 15: Share What God Has Given

1. Barbara Bressi-Donahue, "Friends of the Ring," *Reader's Digest*, June 1999, 154.
2. David Jeremiah, *Acts of Love* (Gresham, OR: Vision House, 1994), 92.
3. Bressi-Donahue, "Friends," 153–60.

Chapter 16: Love Those in Need

1. Gene Weingarten, "Pearls before Breakfast," *Washington Post*, April 8, 2007, https://www.washingtonpost.com/lifestyle/magazine/pearls-before -breakfast-can-one-of-the-nations-great-musicians-cut-through-the-fog -of-a-dc-rush-hour-lets-find-out/2014/09/23/8a6d46da-4331-11e4-b47c -f5889e061e5f_story.html.
2. Frederick Dale Bruner, *The Churchbook: Matthew 13–28* (Dallas: Word Publishing, 1990), 918.
3. David Aikman, *Great Souls: Six Who Changed the Century* (Nashville: Word Publishing, 1998), 199–221, 224.

Chapter 18: Reserve Judgment of Life's Storms

1. Ecclesiastes 7:8.
2. Romans 12:12.
3. Matthew 6:34.

Chapter 20: Listen for the Song of the Whip-poor-will

1. Augustine, *Confessions I.i*, as quoted in Peter Kreeft, *Heaven: The Heart's Deepest Longing* (San Francisco: Ignatius Press, 1989), 49. The inspiration for this essay about the whip-poor-will is drawn from Kreeft's description in "The Nightingale in the Heart," 51–54.
2. With appreciation to Landon Saunders for this idea.
3. Augustine, *Confessions*.

The Lucado Reader's Guide

Discover . . . Inside every book by Max Lucado, you'll find words of encouragement and inspiration that will draw you into a deeper experience with Jesus and treasures for your walk with God. What will you discover?

3:16: The Numbers of Hope
. . . the 26 words that can change your life.
core scripture: John 3:16

And the Angels Were Silent
. . . what Jesus Christ's final days can teach you about what matters most.
core scripture: Matthew 20–27

Anxious for Nothing
. . . be anxious for nothing.
core scripture: Philippians 4:4–8

The Applause of Heaven
. . . the secret to a truly satisfying life.
core scripture: The Beatitudes, Matthew 5:1–10

Before Amen
. . . the power of a simple prayer.
core scripture: Psalm 145:19

Come Thirsty
. . . how to rehydrate your heart and sink into the wellspring of God's love.
core scripture: John 7:37–38

Cure for the Common Life
. . . the unique things God designed you to do with your life.
core scripture: 1 Corinthians 12:7

Facing Your Giants
. . . when God is for you, no challenge is too great.
core scripture: 1 and 2 Samuel

Fearless
. . . how faith is the antidote to the fear in your life.
core scripture: John 14:1, 3

A Gentle Thunder
. . . the God who will do whatever it takes to lead his children back to him.
core scripture: Psalm 81:7

Glory Days
. . . how you fight from victory, not for it.
core scripture: Joshua 21:43–45

God Came Near
. . . a love so great that it left heaven to become part of your world.
core scripture: John 1:14

Grace
. . . the incredible gift that saves and sustains you.
core scripture: Hebrews 12:15

The Great House of God
. . . a blueprint for peace, joy, and love found in the Lord's Prayer.
core scripture: The Lord's Prayer, Matthew 6:9–13

He Chose the Nails
. . . a love so deep that it chose death on a cross—just to win your heart.
core scripture: 1 Peter 1:18–20

He Still Moves Stones
. . . the God who still does the impossible—in your life.
core scripture: Matthew 12:20

In the Eye of the Storm
. . . peace in the storms of your life.
core scripture: John 6

In the Grip of Grace
. . . the greatest gift of all—the grace of God.
core scripture: Romans

It's Not About Me
. . . why focusing on God will make sense of your life.
core scripture: 2 Corinthians 3:18

Just Like Jesus
. . . a life free from guilt, fear, and anxiety.
core scripture: Ephesians 4:23–24

A Love Worth Giving
. . . how living loved frees you to love others.
core scripture: 1 Corinthians 13

Next Door Savior
. . . a God who walked life's hardest trials—and still walks with you through yours.
core scripture: Matthew 16:13–16

No Wonder They Call Him the Savior
. . . hope in the unlikeliest place—upon the cross.
core scripture: Romans 5:15

Outlive Your Life
. . . that a great God created you to do great things.
core scripture: Acts 1

Six Hours One Friday
. . . forgiveness and healing in the middle of loss and failure.
core scripture: John 19–20

Traveling Light
. . . the power to release the burdens you were never meant to carry.
core scripture: Psalm 23

Unshakable Hope
. . . God has given us his very great and precious promises.
core scripture: 2 Peter 1:4

When God Whispers Your Name
. . . the path to hope in knowing that God knows you, never forgets you, and cares about the details of your life.
core scripture: John 10:3

You'll Get Through This
. . . hope in the midst of your hard times and a God who uses the mess of life for good.
core scripture: Genesis 50:20

Recommended reading if you're struggling with . . .

FEAR AND WORRY

Anxious for Nothing
Before Amen
Come Thirsty
Fearless
For the Tough Times
Next Door Savior
Traveling Light

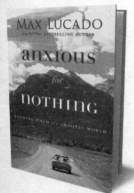

DISCOURAGEMENT

He Still Moves Stones
Next Door Savior

GRIEF/DEATH OF A LOVED ONE

Next Door Savior
Traveling Light
When Christ Comes
When God Whispers Your Name
You'll Get Through This

GUILT

In the Grip of Grace
Just Like Jesus

LONELINESS

God Came Near

SIN

Before Amen
Facing Your Giants
He Chose the Nails
Six Hours One Friday

WEARINESS

Before Amen
When God Whispers Your Name
You'll Get Through This

Recommended reading if you want to know more about . . .

THE CROSS

And the Angels Were Silent
He Chose the Nails
No Wonder They Call Him the Savior
Six Hours One Friday

GRACE

Before Amen
Grace
He Chose the Nails
In the Grip of Grace

HEAVEN

The Applause of Heaven
When Christ Comes

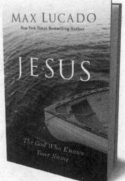

SHARING THE GOSPEL

God Came Near
Grace
No Wonder They Call Him the Savior

Recommended reading if you're looking for more . . .

COMFORT

For the Tough Times
He Chose the Nails
Next Door Savior
Traveling Light
You'll Get Through This

COMPASSION

Outlive Your Life

COURAGE

Facing Your Giants
Fearless

HOPE

3:16: The Numbers of Hope
Before Amen
Facing Your Giants
A Gentle Thunder
God Came Near
Grace
Unshakable Hope

JOY

The Applause of Heaven
Cure for the Common Life
When God Whispers Your Name

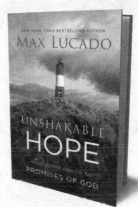

LOVE

Come Thirsty
A Love Worth Giving
No Wonder They Call Him the Savior

PEACE

And the Angels Were Silent
Anxious for Nothing
Before Amen
The Great House of God
In the Eye of the Storm
Traveling Light
You'll Get Through This

SATISFACTION

And the Angels Were Silent
Come Thirsty
Cure for the Common Life
Great Day Every Day

TRUST

A Gentle Thunder
It's Not About Me
Next Door Savior

Max Lucado books make great gifts!

If you're coming up to a special occasion, consider one of these.

FOR ADULTS:

Anxious for Nothing
For the Tough Times
Grace for the Moment
Live Loved
The Lucado Life Lessons Study Bible
Mocha with Max
DaySpring Daybrighteners® and cards

FOR TEENS/GRADUATES:

Let the Journey Begin
You Can Be Everything God Wants You to Be
You Were Made to Make a Difference

FOR KIDS:

I'm Not a Scaredy Cat
Just in Case You Ever Wonder
The Oak Inside the Acorn
You Are Special

FOR PASTORS AND TEACHERS:

God Thinks You're Wonderful
You Changed My Life

AT CHRISTMAS:

Because of Bethlehem
The Crippled Lamb
The Christmas Candle
God Came Near